# Sing the Psalms
## *SIMPLY*

A RESPONSORIAL PSALTER
FOR SUNDAYS & SOLEMNITIES

*TEXT:* GRAIL PSALTER 1963

*MUSIC:* JOHN AINSLIE

KEYBOARD EDITION

BENEDICAMUS

Published in 2015 by

BENEDICAMUS

76 Great Bushey Drive, London N20 8QL, UK

ISBN: 978-0-9929050-4-0

Companion Edition also available:

Cantor & Guitar Edition – ISBN: 978-0-9929050-3-3

# CONTENTS

# INTRODUCTION

The Psalms are the Bible's song book. They are the inspired word of God. In their proclamation, God speaks – or rather sings – to his people, and through them God is worshipped by his people in the words he inspired.

The psalms have been a primary resource in the Christian liturgy throughout its history. In the early Church they were sung by a psalmist, with everyone listening. In the Mass, the 'gradual psalm' was similarly sung with a people's response; later this became the musically complex Graduals, reserved to trained singers.

In the revision of the Lectionary following the Second Vatican Council, the 'gradual psalm' was reinstated as the Responsorial Psalm. 'As a rule it is to be sung' by the 'psalmist or cantor of the psalm' as 'an integral part of the Liturgy of the Word' – so says the *Introduction to the Lectionary*. It is therefore proclaimed from the ambo or lectern reserved for the proclamation of the word of God.

Ideally, each psalm setting should be a lyrical expression of every line – even every word – of each psalm, to convey to the listeners its full content. But that is a counsel of perfection. Few churches have musicians with the skills or time to rehearse and perform a different through-composed setting each Sunday. A collection of psalm-settings with this scope is projected as *Sing the Psalms Lyrically*.

*Sing the Psalms Simply* provides settings of the Responsorial Psalms in which the psalm text is set to simple psalm-tones – but tones specially composed to reflect the overall sense of the psalm, be it of praise or prayer. It is intended to make the singing of the psalm practical for cantors with little experience.

The settings of the response to the psalm are deliberately rhythmical, in order to facilitate the people's vocal participation. However, it should be noted that the response is secondary to the proclamation of the psalm itself – and indeed, the psalm may be sung *in directum* by the cantor, without the response.

I am very grateful to Paul Wellicome, who has advised on guitar accompaniment and provided introductory guidance for guitarists, and to Paul Inwood, who has done the same for the keyboard accompaniments and accompanists, as well as proof-reading both editions. (Any remaining errors are entirely my fault.) I am also grateful to the Composers' Forum of the Society of Saint Gregory for its support and encouragement.

John Ainslie

# CANTORS: HOW TO SING THE PSALMS

**Cardinal principle**

> **It is essential that the psalm texts in this book are sung with the natural rhythms and accentuation of spoken English.**

This requires good diction, so that the text of the psalm is communicated to the congregation clearly enough for them to make it their prayer. The natural tendency when singing a text on a reciting note is to level out the natural rhythms of the text: this must be resisted.

For the same reason, the cantor must avoid slowing up the tempo when singing the cadence of a line. Sometimes the preparatory notes of a cadence will coincide with the accentuation of the words, sometimes they won't. The text must always govern the accentuation.

Where a response text is duplicated at the beginning of a psalm verse, the repetition in the psalm is noted as 'optional' – or it is omitted altogether. If such a psalm is sung without the response, it must be re-incorporated in the psalm.

The psalmist should be both humbled and encouraged by the words of the late Dom Ambrose Tinsley, monk of Glenstal Abbey, Ireland (from his *Wisely, Pray the Psalms*, p. 69 – with editorial addition):

> The spirit prays in us. Of course we pray as well. We say our words and, when we use the psalms, we say the ancient hallowed words that have been lovingly passed down to us... And so, before we even start a psalm and certainly when we are reading [*Ed.* or singing!] it, we need to let that Spirit come and lead us through the psalm-words until we become... the image and the likeness of the One from whom the Spirit, and the Word itself, have come.

# KEYBOARD PLAYERS: HOW TO ACCOMPANY THE PSALMS

## Paul Inwood

The keyboard player's task in the Responsorial Psalm is a twofold one: to lead or accompany the Response, and to accompany the cantor in the psalm tone. Each requires a slightly different approach.

In the Response, the first thing that will happen at the beginning of the psalm will be a playover or introduction. Generally speaking, the best thing to do is to play the melody only in octaves (the written pitch + an octave below) or in single notes, *mezzo forte*. (Having the melody alone, unencumbered by the harmonies, makes it easier for the people to hear.) The cantor then sings the Response while the player accompanies with the harmonies provided, using an appropriate supporting registration and volume. Then the people will sing the Response, while the player accompanies with the harmonies using a more substantial registration and volume.

Between the psalm verses, the player will accompany the people in the response using the more substantial registration, but will watch for any gestural directions to the people from the cantor. For the verses, once again using a quieter registration, the player will underpin what the cantor sings.

Below you will find some notes about organ registrations and on the use of other keyboard instruments.

### What to play

Even for an accomplished accompanist, one of the most difficult things to do is keep in absolute synchronisation with a solo singer (in this case the cantor), especially as the singer will be using natural speech rhythm rather than strictly-metred time (see the notes for cantors above). This book makes it much easier for the player by distinguishing what the player plays from what the cantor sings.

The basic rule for the psalm tones is this: **play only the semibreves and stemless minims. Do not play anything else!** The cantor's 'black' notes are provided at a smaller size for your guidance, and for any cantors who may be singing from this accompaniment edition. The length of all notes is entirely dependent on the text rhythm established and sung by the cantor.

Thus the following line:

1. O give the Lord you            sons of    God,      give the Lord          glory    and power;
2. The Lord's voice resounding  on    the   waters,   the Lord on the im-mensity  of  waters;
3. The God of                       glo - ry  thunders.  In his temple they  all          cry: 'Glory!'

should be interpreted thus by the cantor:

1. O give the Lord you            sons of    God,      give the Lord          glo -ry    and power;
2. The Lord's voice resounding  on   the   waters,   the Lord on the im-men-si-ty  of  waters;
3. The God of                       glo - ry  thunders.  In his temple they   all          cry: 'Glory!'

and thus by the accompanist:

1. O give the Lord you            sons  of    God,      give the Lord          glory    and power;
2. The Lord's voice resounding  on    the   waters,   the Lord on the im-mensity  of  waters;
3. The God of                       glo - ry  thunders.  In his temple they  all          cry: 'Glory!'

Why is this? Because trying to play the black notes at the exact same time as the cantor will tend to fail, and the accompanist will then 'get in the way' of the singer by being out of sync. Also, every singer has their own individual speech rhythms which may not always be absolutely identical with other people's. Much easier just to put down the first chord in each bar and then watch where to change to the next chord, rather than trying to follow each twist and turn of the cantor's melody. It also makes the playing nicely *legato*.

Notice, too, what is said to cantors above about not slowing down at cadences (i.e. at the end of each bar). Note, too, where an accented preparatory cadence (as at 'glory and' above) requires additional notes for the cantor for some verses but not for others.

Another way in which this book makes the task of the keyboard player easier is in the harmonisations. While these do not always respect the strictest rules of musical grammar, they do generally lie easily under the fingers. More experienced players should feel free to adapt harmonisations where desired.

Very occasionally an interval of a 9th or 10th will be found in the left hand (lower stave). When this happens, the player will always be able to take the higher note(s) with the right hand. Do it! Sharing between the hands is part of good keyboard technique, and you may also find instances where it can be easier to play some right-hand stave notes with the left hand.

## Registrations and keyboard instruments

All organs, whether pipe or electronic, are different. The following is only for guidance and will need adapting to individual circumstances.

To accompany the cantor, an 8ft flute or flutes at 8 and 4ft pitch on the Swell or Choir will usually be sufficient. The 4ft will help tuning. A more penetrating sound, such as an 8ft Dulciana or Salicional may be useful too, but some Salicionals and Gambas can be very acidic.

For the congregation, it's important to remember that the psalm is more in the nature of a meditation after the First Reading and not a hymn. Diapason and principal stops will often be too loud for the Response, except in the most joyful ones. Better to use a Great 8ft flute, coupled through to the Swell, perhaps adding a Great 4ft flute as the psalm progresses.

All of the music in this book has been written for manuals only, and in some cases adding pedals will adversely affect the feel of the music. In general, only use pedals in the Response, and even then judiciously.

If no organ is available, all this music will work on piano or electronic keyboard. On the piano, the player can use touch to differentiate between the volume needed for cantor and that for people. Try occasionally playing an octave higher (e.g. quietly during a psalm verse). Playing the bass line of the Response in octaves will sometimes be effective in the hands of more experienced players.

Electronic pianos and keyboards frequently have organ sounds that are not very pleasant and sound too much like full organ to be useful for accompanying psalms and other quiet pieces. Better to use a nice Grand Piano sound or, on some keyboards, a flute or harp sound can be useful. On a piano, play harder for more volume in the Response. On a keyboard, there may be a swell pedal to alter the volume. Unless you are an expert, it is better not to try to change sounds between psalm tone and Response, which can become fussy and risks holding up the progression of the music.

## Guitar and/or keyboard

All the music in this book has been designed to be played on the keyboard. The companion volume contains melody lines only and chord symbols for the use of parish guitarists. **These chords are usually quite different and cannot normally be used together with the keyboard accompaniment**. If no guitars are available, use keyboard throughout. If no keyboard is available, use guitars throughout. If you have both at your disposal, one possibility is to use guitar in the psalm verses and keyboard for the Response.

# BOOK 1

PSALMS 1 – 40 (41)

# Psalm 1 – Blessed indeed is the one who trusts in the Lord

vv. 1-4, 6. R/ Ps 39:5

> 6th Sunday in Ordinary Time (Year C)
> St David (March 1 – in Wales)

*Response:* **Hap-py the man who has    placed his trust in the    Lord.**

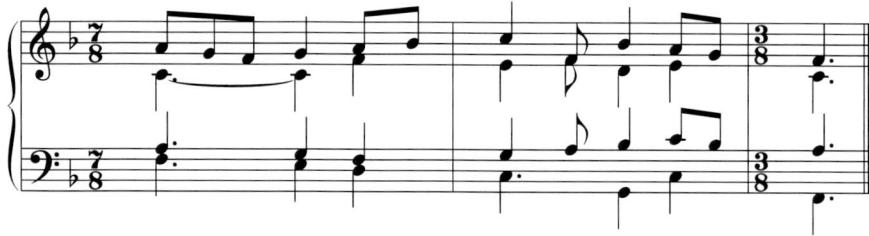

1.  Happy indeed is the man        who follows not the counsel of the wicked;      nor lingers in the way of sinners

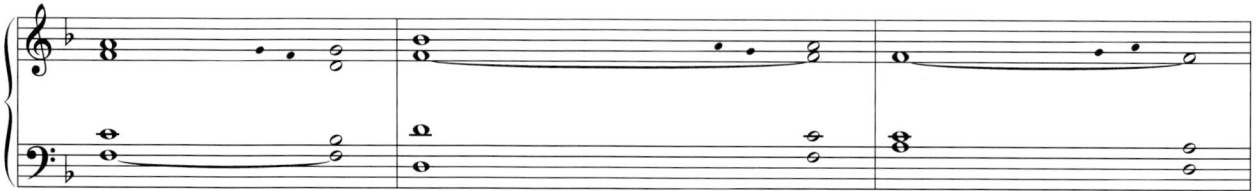

nor sits in the compa-ny of scorners,     but whose delight is the law of the Lord

and who ponders his law day and night.

2.  He is like a tree that is planted      beside the flow-ing waters,

that yields its fruit in due season    and whose leaves shall ne-ver fade;      and all that he does shall prosper.

3. Not so are the wicked, not so!     For they like winnowed chaff shall be driven away by the wind.

For the Lord guards the way of the just     but the way of the wicked leads to doom.

# Psalm 4 – When I call, answer me, O God

vv. 2, 4, 7, 9. R/ v. 4

3rd Sunday of Easter (Year B)

*Response:* **Lift up the light of your face on us, O Lord.**

1. When I call, answer me, O               God  of justice;
2. It is the Lord who grants favours to those whom he  loves;
3. 'What can bring us happiness?'          ma - ny  say.
4. I will lie down in peace and sleep       comes at  once,

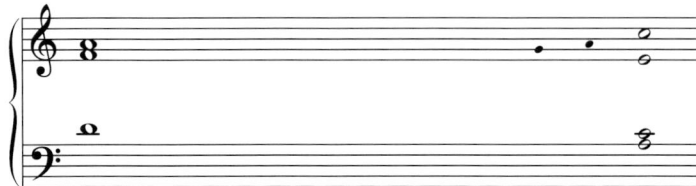

from anguish you released me, have  mer - cy and hear me!
the Lord hears me when        -     ev - er  I   call him.
Lift up the light of your face on      us,____ O    Lord.
for you alone, Lord, make me       dwell____ in  safety.

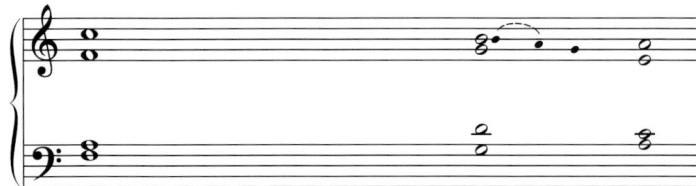

# Psalm 8 - O Lord, our Lord, how majestic is your name!

vv. 4-9. R/ v. 2

Trinity Sunday (Year C)

*Response:* How great is your name, O Lord___ our God, through all___ the earth!___

1. When I see the heavens, the work    of    your hands,    the moon and the stars which you ar-ranged,
2. Yet you have made him little less    than    a    god,    with glory and hon    -    our you crowned him,
3. All of them,    sheep and cattle,    yes, even the    sav-age beasts,

what is man that you should keep him  in  mind,    mortal man that you    care  for  him?
gave him power over the works    of  your hand,    put all things un  -  der  his  feet.
birds of the    air,  and  fish    that make their way  through the waters.

# Psalm 14 (15) – Lord, who shall dwell in your presence?

vv. 2-5. R/ cf Ps 114 (116) v.9

22nd Sunday in Ordinary Time (Year B)
16th Sunday in Ordinary Time (Year C)

*Response:* **The just will live in the pre-sence of the Lord.**

1. Lord, who shall dwell on your ho-ly mountain? He who walks with-out fault,

*On 22nd Sunday in O.T.*

he who acts with justice and speaks the truth from his heart.

*On 16th Sunday in O.T.*

he who acts with justice and speaks the truth from his heart; he who does not slander with his tongue.

2. He who does no wrong to his brother, who casts no slur on his neighbour,
3. He who keeps his pledge, come what may; who takes no interest on a loan

who holds the godless in dis - dain, but honours those who fear the Lord.
and accepts no bribes a-gainst the innocent. Such a man will stand firm for ever.

6

# Psalm 15 (16) – O Lord, it is you who are my portion and cup

## EXTRACT A – vv. 5, 8-11. R/ v. 1

Easter Vigil (after 2nd reading)
33rd Sunday in Ordinary Time (Year B)

*Response:* **Pre - serve me, God, I take re-fuge in you.**

1. O Lord, it is you who are my por-tion and cup;     it is you yourself who are my     prize.
2. And so my heart rejoices, my     soul is glad;     even my body shall     rest in     safety.
3. You will show me the     path of life,     the fullness of joy     in your presence,

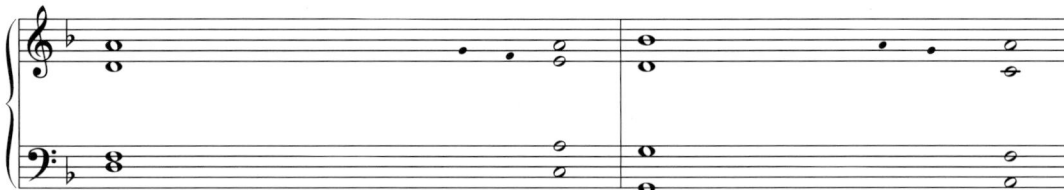

I keep the Lord ever     in my sight:     since he is at my right hand, I shall stand firm.
For you will not leave my soul a-mong the dead,     nor let your beloved     know de - cay.
[     ]     at your right hand happi - ness for ever.

*omit in verse 3*

7

## EXCERPT B – vv. 1-2, 5, 7-11

3rd Sunday of Easter (Year A) – response 1 (v. 11)
13th Sunday in Ordinary Time (Year C) - response 2 (cf v. 5)

*Response 1 (3rd Sunday of Easter):*

**Show us, Lord, the path of life.**

*Response 2 (13th Sunday in O.T.):*

**O Lord, it is you who are my por--tion.**

1. Preserve me, God, I take re - fuge in you.    I say to the Lord: 'You are my God.'
2. I will bless the Lord who gives me counsel,    who even at night di - rects my heart.
3. And so my heart rejoices, my soul is glad;    even my body shall rest in safety.
4. You will show me the path of life,    the fullness of joy in your presence,

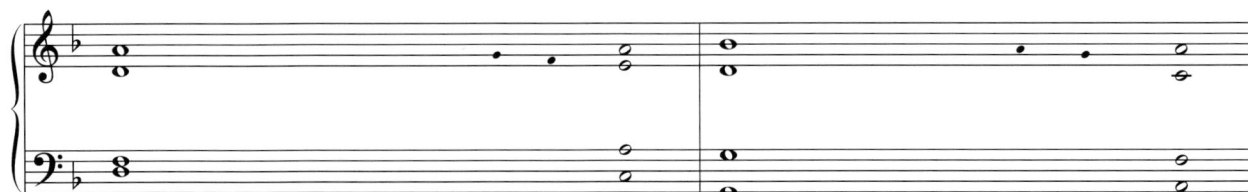

O Lord, it is you who are my por - tion and cup;    it is you yourself who are my prize.
I keep the Lord ever in my sight:    since he is at my right hand, I shall stand firm.
For you will not leave my soul a - mong the dead,    nor let your beloved know de - cay.
[             ]    at your right hand happi - ness for ever.

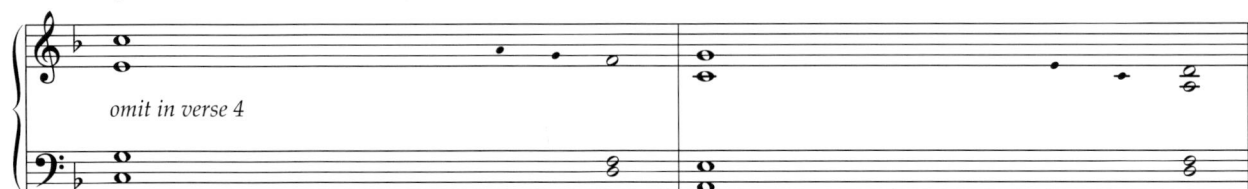

*omit in verse 4*

8

# Psalm 16 (17) – O Lord, hear a cause that is just

vv. 1, 5-6, 8, 15. R/ v. 15

32nd Sunday in Ordinary Time (Year C)

*Response:* I shall be filled, when I a - wake, with the sight of your glo-ry, O Lord.

1. Lord, hear a cause that is just, pay heed to my cry.
2. I kept my feet firmly in your paths; there was no faltering in my steps.
3. Guard me as the apple of your eye. Hide me in the shadow of your wings.

Turn your ear to my prayer: no deceit is on my lips.
I am here and I call, you will hear me, O God. Turn your ear to me, hear my words.
As for me, in my justice I shall see your face and be filled, when I awake, with the sight of your glory.

# Psalm 17 (18) – I love you, Lord, my strength

vv. 2-4, 47, 51. R/ v. 2

30th Sunday in Ordinary Time (Year A)
31st Sunday in Ordinary Time (Year B)

*Response:* **I love you, Lord, my strength,__ I love you, Lord, my__ strength.**

*The psalmist continues:*

1. ...my rock, my for-tress, my saviour.

My God is the rock where I take refuge;   my shield, my mighty help, my stronghold.

The Lord is worthy of all praise:   when I call I am saved from my foes.

2. Long life to the Lord   my rock!   Praised be the God who saves me.

He has given great victories to his king   and shown his love for his   a-nointed.

10

# Psalm 18 (19) – Praise of God, the law-giver

## EXTRACT A – vv. 8-11. R/ Jn 6:69

> 3rd Sunday of Lent (Year B) – response version 1
> Common Psalm 1 for Ordinary Time – response version 1
> Easter Vigil (after the 6th reading) – response version 2
> Pentecost Vigil (after the 2nd reading, alt.) – response version 2

*Response Version 1 (3rd Sunday of Lent & Ordinary Time):*

**You, Lord, have the mes-sage of e - ter - - nal life.**

*Response Version 2 (Easter & Pentecost Vigils):*

**You have the mes-sage of e - ter - - nal life, O Lord.**

1. The law of the Lord is perfect, it re - vives the soul.
2. The precepts of the Lord are right, they glad - den the heart.
3. The fear of the Lord is holy, abid - ing for ever.
4. They are more to be de-sired than gold, than the pu -rest of gold

The rule of the Lord is to be trusted, it gives wisdom to the simple.
The command of the Lord is clear, it gives light to the eyes.
The decrees of the Lord are truth and all of them just.
and sweeter are they than honey, than honey from the comb.

## EXTRACT B – vv. 8-11. R/ v. 9

> 15th Sunday in Ordinary Time (Year C) (alternative)

*Response:* **The pre-cepts of the Lord glad- den the heart.**

*Verses as above for Extract A*

# PSALM 18 (19)

## EXTRACT C – vv. 8-10, 15. R/ Jn 6:63

3rd Sunday in Ordinary Time (Year C)

*Response:* **Your words are spi-rit, Lord, and they are life.**

1. The law of the Lord is perfect, it re - vives the soul.
2. The precepts of the Lord are right, they glad - den the heart.
3. The fear of the Lord is holy, abid - ing for ever.
4. May the spoken words of my mouth, the thoughts of my heart,

The rule of the Lord is to be trusted, it gives wisdom to the simple.
The command of the Lord is clear, it gives light to the eyes.
The decrees of the Lord are truth and all of them just.
win favour in your sight, O Lord, my rescu - er, my rock.

## EXTRACT D – vv. 8, 10, 12-14. R/ v. 9

26th Sunday in Ordinary Time (Year B)

*Response:* **The pre-cepts of the Lord glad- den the heart.**

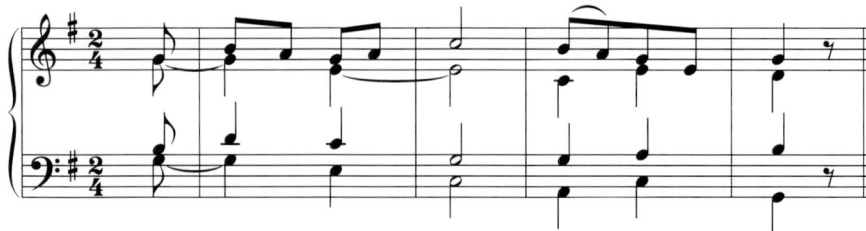

1. The law of the Lord is perfect, it re - vives the soul.
2. The fear of the Lord is holy, abid - ing for ever.
3. So in them your servant finds in - struction; great reward is in their keeping.
4. From presumption re - strain your servant and let it not rule me.

## PSALM 18 (19)

The rule of the Lord is to be trusted, it gives wisdom to the simple.
The decrees of the Lord are truth and all of them just.
But who can detect all his errors? From hidden faults ac - quit me.
Then I shall be blameless, clean from grave sin.

EXTRACT E – vv. 2-5. R/ v. 3

SS. Peter & Paul (Vigil – June 28)

*Response:* **Their word goes forth___ through all___ the earth.**

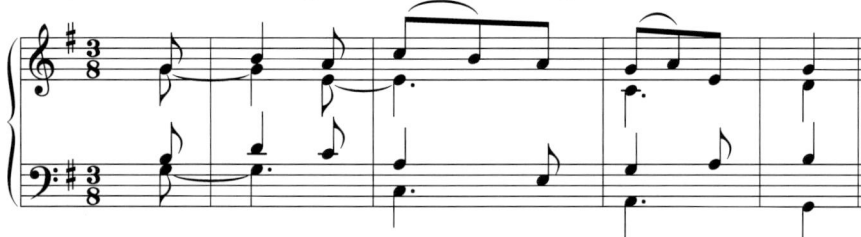

1. The hea- vens pro- claim the glo - ry of God and the firmament shows forth the work of his hands.

Day unto day takes up the story and night unto night makes known the message.

2. No speech, no word, no voice is heard yet their span extends through all the earth,

their words to the utmost bounds of the world.

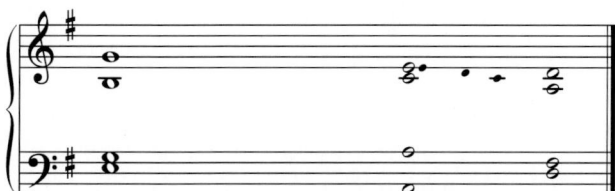

# Psalm 21 (22) – My God, my God, why have you forsaken me?

EXTRACT A – vv. 8-9, 17-20, 23-24. R/ v. 2

> Palm Sunday of the Passion of the Lord
> Common Psalm for Holy Week

Response: My God, my God, why have you for - sa - - ken me?

1. All who see me de - ride me. They curl their lips, they toss their heads.
2. Many dogs have sur-rounded me, a band of the wick - ed be - set me.
3. They divide my cloth -ing a - mong them. They cast lots for my robe.

'He trusted in the Lord, let him save him; let him release him if this is his friend.'
They tear holes in my hands and my feet. I can count every one of my bones.
O Lord, do not leave me a - lone, my strength, make haste to help me!

4. I will tell of your name to my brethren and praise you where they are as-sembled.

'You who fear the Lord give him praise; all sons of Jacob, give him glory. Revere him, Is -ra-el's sons.'

# PSALM 21 (22)

## EXTRACT B – vv. 26-28, 30-32. R/ v. 26

5th Sunday of Easter (Year B)

*Response:* **You, Lord, are my praise in the great___ as - sem--bly.**

1. My vows I will pay before          those who fear him.
2. All the earth shall remember and return to the Lord,
3. And my soul shall live for him, my child - ren serve him.

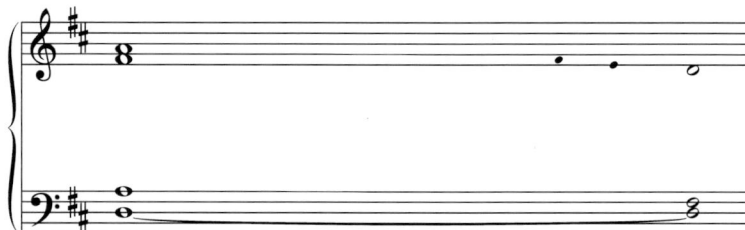

The poor shall eat and shall        have their fill.
all families of the nations wor    -    ship be - fore him.
They shall tell of the Lord to generations yet to come,

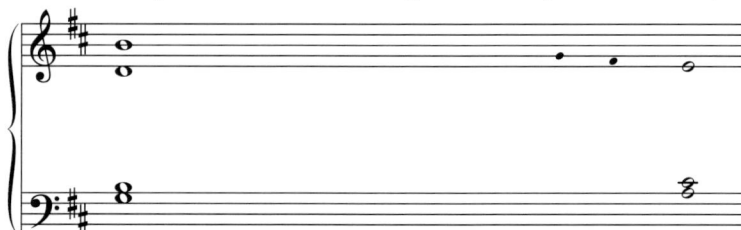

They shall praise the Lord,        those who seek him.
They shall worship him, all the mighty of the earth;
declare his faithfulness to peoples   yet un - born:

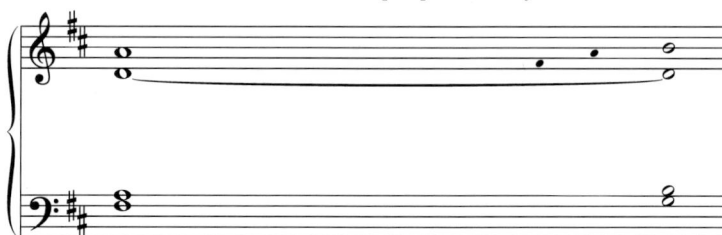

May their hearts live for ev    -    er and ever.
before him shall bow all who go down to the dust.
'These things the         Lord has done.'

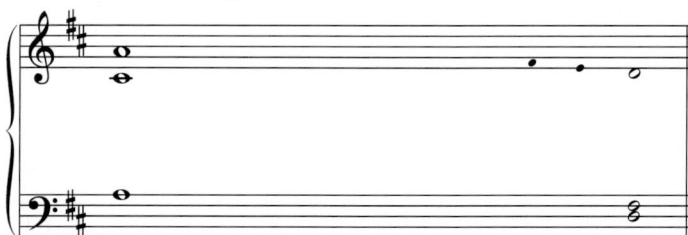

# Psalm 22 (23) – The Lord is my shepherd

4th Sunday of Lent (Year A) - response 1
4th Sunday of Easter (Year A) - response 1
28th Sunday in Ordinary Time (Year A) - response 2

Christ the King (Year A)* - response 1
16th Sunday in Ordinary Time (Year B) - response 1
Sacred Heart (Year C) - response 1

*Response 1 (all except 28th Sunday in O.T.):*

The Lord is my shep--herd;_____ there is no-thing I shall want.

*Response 2 (28th Sunday in O.T.):*

In the Lord's own_ house_ shall I dwell for ev - er and ev - er.

*\* - In verse 2, the Lectionary omits 'If I should... fear' on the solemnity of Christ the King. It is suggested that these words be retained.*

1. The Lord is my shepherd; there is nothing I shall want.
2. He guides me a-long the right path; he is true to his name.

Fresh and green are the pastures where he gives me re-pose.
If I should walk in the val-ley of darkness, no evil would I fear.

Near restful wa - ters he leads me to revive my droop-ing spirit.
You are there with your crook and your staff; with these you give me comfort.

16

# PSALM 22 (23)

3. You have prepared a ban-quet for me      in the sight of my foes.
4. Surely goodness and kind-ness shall follow me    all the days of my life.

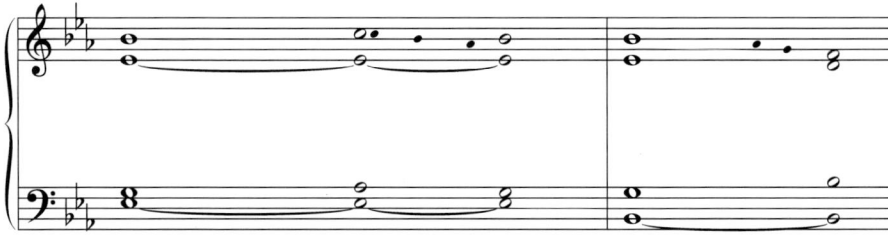

My head you have anoin-ted with oil;      my cup is ov - er-flowing.
In the Lord's own house shall I dwell      for ev - er and ever.

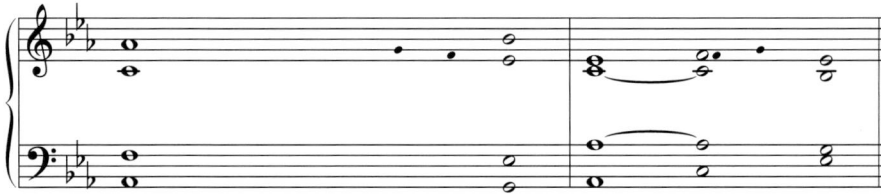

17

# Psalm 23 (24) – The Lord's is the earth and its fullness

## EXTRACT A – vv. 1-6

4th Sunday of Advent (Year A) – response 1 (cf vv. 7, 10)
All Saints – response 2 (cf v. 6)

*Response 1:*
*4th Sunday*
*of Advent*

Let the Lord_ en--ter! He is the king_ of_ glo--ry.

*Response 2:*
*All Saints*

Such **are the** / **are__** **men** / **those** who seek your face, O__ Lord.

1. The Lord's is the earth       and   its fullness,   the world and          all   its   peoples.
2. Who shall climb the mountain  of    the Lord?       Who shall stand in his ho - ly   place?
3. He shall receive blessings    from  the Lord        and reward from the God who saves him.

It is he who set it                on   the    seas;   on the waters he    made  it   firm.
The man with clean hands  and  pure  heart   who desires not    worth-less things.
*Either:* Such are                 those who seek him,  seek the face of the God   of Jacob.
*or:* Such are the                 men  who seek him,   seek the face of the God   of Jacob.

18

## EXTRACT B – vv. 7-10. R/ v. 8

The Presentation of the Lord (February 2)

*Response:* **Who is the king of glo - - ry?**     **It is the Lord.**

1. O gates, lift    high your heads;    grow higher, an  -  cient doors.    Let him enter, the king    of glory.
2. Who is the      king of glory?      The Lord, the mighty,  the valiant,    the Lord, the           valiant in war.
3. O gates, lift    high your heads;    grow higher, an  -  cient doors.    Let him enter, the king    of glory.
4. Who is he, the king  of  glory?     He, the          Lord      of  armies,    he is the                king    of glory.

# Psalm 24 (25) – To you, O Lord, I lift up my soul

## EXTRACT A – vv. 4-9

26th Sunday in Ordinary Time (Year A) – response 1 (v. 6)
3rd Sunday in Ordinary Time (Year B) – response 2 (v. 4)
1st Sunday of Lent (Year B) – response 3 (cf v. 10)

*Response 1 (26th Sunday in O.T.):*

Re - mem-ber your mer- - cy, Lord._

*Response 2 (3rd Sunday in O.T.):*

Lord, make me know_ your_ ways.

*Response 3 (1st Sunday of Lent):*

Your ways, O Lord, are faith-ful-ness and love for those who keep_ your_ co-ve-nant.

1. Lord, make me know your ways. Lord, teach me your paths.

Make me walk in your truth, and teach me: for you are God my saviour.

2. Remember your mer-cy, Lord, and the love you have shown from of old.

*This line is sung on 26th Sunday in Ordinary Time only*

Do not remember the sins of my youth.

In your love re-mem-ber me,       because of your good-ness, O Lord.

3.   The Lord is good and upright.     He shows the path to those___who stray,

he guides the humble  in the right path;   he teaches his way to the poor.

# PSALM 24 (25)

## EXTRACT B – vv. 4-5, 8-9, 10, 14. R/ v. 1

> 1st Sunday of Advent (Year C)
> Common Psalm 1 for Advent

*Response:* **To you, O Lord, I lift up my soul.**

**Verses 1 & 3:**

1. Lord, make me know your ways. Lord, teach me your paths.
3. His ways are faithful -ness and love for those who keep his cov'-nant and will.

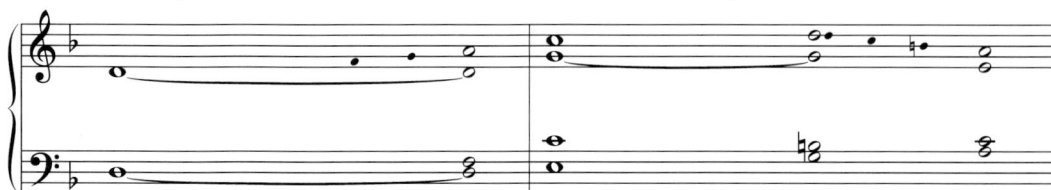

Make me walk in your truth, and teach me: for you are God my saviour.
The Lord's friendship is for those who re-vere him; to them he re-veals his covenant.

**Verse 2:**

2. The Lord is good and upright. He shows the path to those who stray,

he guides the humble in the right path; he teaches his way to the poor.

# Psalm 26 (27) – The Lord is my light and my salvation

EXTRACT A – vv. 1, 4, 7-8. R/ v. 13

7th Sunday of Easter (Year A)

*Response:*   I am   sure I shall see the Lord's   good - - ness in the   land of the   liv - - ing.

*Verses 1 & 3*

1. The Lord is my light and   my help;   whom shall I   fear?
3. O Lord, hear my voice when I   call;   have mercy and answer.

The Lord is the stronghold of my   life;   before whom shall I   shrink?
Of you my heart   has spoken: 'Seek   his   face.'

*Verse 2*   There is one thing I ask of the Lord,   for this I long,   to live in the house of the Lord,

all the days of my life,   to savour the sweetness of the Lord,   to behold his temple.

# PSALM 26 (27)

## EXTRACT B – vv. 1, 4, 13-14. R/ v. 1

3rd Sunday in Ordinary Time (Year A)
Common Psalm 2 for Ordinary Time

*Response:* **The Lord is my light and my help.**

**Verses 1 & 3**

1. [                                                    ] whom shall I fear?
3. I am sure I shall see the Lord's goodness in the land of the living.

*Omit first phrase of verse 1*

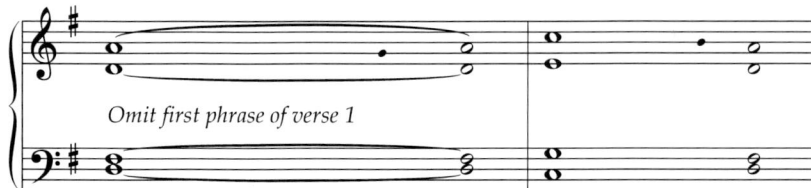

The Lord is the stronghold of my life; before whom shall I shrink?
Hope in him, hold firm and take heart. Hope in the Lord.

**Verse 2** There is one thing I ask of the Lord, for this I long, to live in the house of the Lord,

all the days of my life, to savour the sweetness of the Lord, to behold his temple.

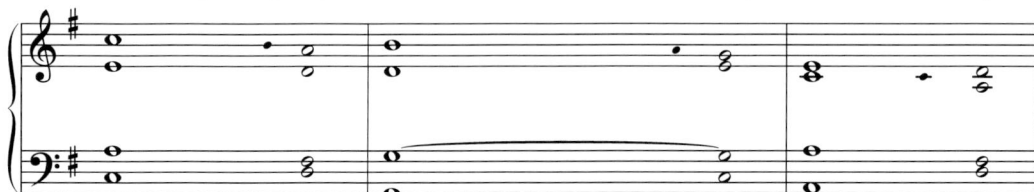

# PSALM 26 (27)

## EXTRACT C – vv. 1, 7-9, 13-14. R/ v. 1

2nd Sunday of Lent (Year C)

*Response:* **The Lord is my light and my help.**___

*The cantor continues...*

1. ...whom shall I fear?     The Lord is the stronghold of my life;     before whom shall I shrink?

2. O Lord, hear my voice when     I     call;     have mercy     and  answer.
3. It is your face, O Lord, that     I     seek;     hide not     your   face.
4. I am sure I shall see the     Lord's goodness     in the land of  the   living.

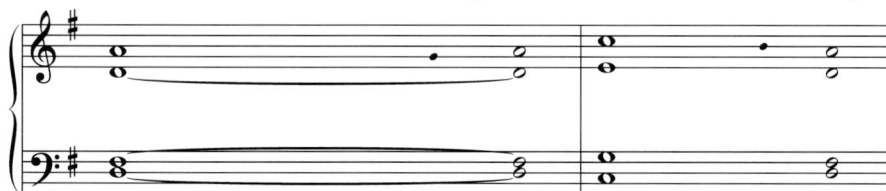

Of you my heart               has spoken:  'Seek          his face.'
Dismiss not your servant     in     anger;  you have been my help.
Hope in him, hold firm and take  heart.     Hope in        the Lord.

25

## EXTRACT D – vv. 1, 4, 7-9, 13-14 R/ v. 1 or v. 13

All Souls (November 2)

*Response:* **The Lord is my light and my help.**

*Alternative*
*Response:* **I am sure I shall see the Lord's good - - ness in the land of the liv - - ing.**

### Verses 1, 3 & 4

1. [The Lord is my light and my help;] whom shall I fear?
3. O Lord, hear my voice when I call; have mercy and answer.
4. I am sure I shall see the Lord's goodness in the land of the living.

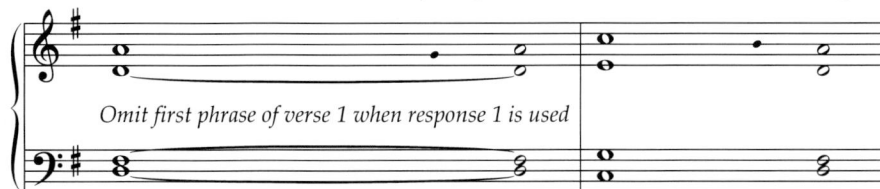

*Omit first phrase of verse 1 when response 1 is used*

The Lord is the stronghold of my life; before whom shall I shrink?
Of you my heart has spoken: 'Seek his face.'
Hope in him, hold firm and take heart. Hope in the Lord.

**Verse 2** There is one thing I ask of the Lord, for this I long, to live in the house of the Lord,

all the days of my life, to savour the sweetness of the Lord, to behold his temple.

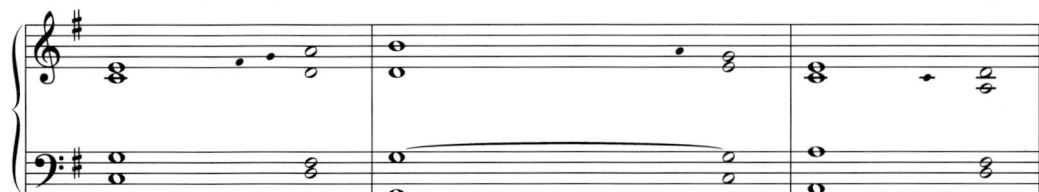

# Psalm 28 (29) – Ascribe to the Lord glory and power

vv. 1-4, 9-10. R/ v. 11

Baptism of the Lord (Year A)

*Response:* **The Lord will bless his peo-ple with peace.**

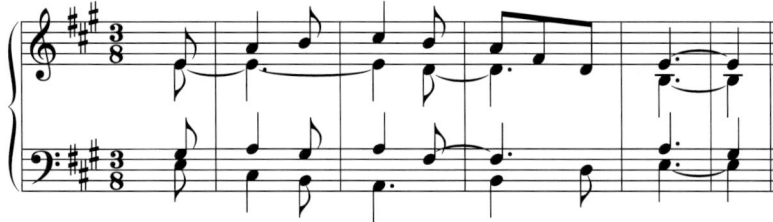

1. O give the Lord you        sons  of    God,      give the Lord      glory   and power;
2. The Lord's voice resounding  on    the  waters,    the Lord on the im-mensity  of  waters;
3. The God of              glo - ry  thunders.  In his temple they all       cry: 'Glory!'

give the Lord the        glory  of  his  name.   Adore the Lord in his  ho - ly    court.
the voice of the          Lord, full  of  power,   the voice of the Lord,  full  of splendour.
The Lord sat enthroned ov  -  er  the  flood;   the Lord sits as        king for    ever.

27

# Psalm 29 (30) – I will thank you, Lord, you have drawn me up

vv. 2, 4-6, 11-13. R/ v. 2

Easter Vigil (after the 4th reading)
3rd Sunday of Easter (Year C)
13th Sunday in Ordinary Time (Year B)
10th Sunday in Ordinary Time (Year C)

*Response:* **I will praise** you, Lord, you have res - -cued me.

*In verse 1, the psalmist continues:*

1. [                          ]  ...and have not let my enemies re-joice ov-er me.
2. Sing psalms to the Lord, you who love him,   give thanks to his   ho - -ly name.
3. The Lord listened   and had   pity.   The Lord   came to my help.

*Omit this phrase in verse 1*

O Lord, you have raised my soul   from the   dead,
His anger lasts but a moment, his fa - vour through   life.
For me you have changed my mourning in - to   dancing,

restored me to life from those who sink in - to   the grave.
At night there are tears, but joy   comes with dawn.
O Lord my God, I will thank   you   for ever.

28

# Psalm 30 (31) – In you, O Lord, I take refuge

EXTRACT A – vv. 2, 6, 12-13, 15-17, 25. R/ Lk 23:46

Good Friday

*Note: It is recommended that on Good Friday the psalm should be sung unaccompanied.*

*Response:* **Fa-ther, in-to your hands I com - mend_ my_ spi-rit.**

*Verses 1 & 3*

1. In you, O Lord, I take refuge. Let me never be put to shame. In your justice set me free.
3. Those who see me in the street run far a - way from me. I am like a dead man,

Into your hands I com-mend my spirit. It is you who will re - deem me, Lord.
forgotten in men's hearts, like a thing thrown a - way.

*Verses 2, 4 & 5*

2. In the face of all my foes I am a re - proach,
4. But as for me, I trust in you, Lord, I say: 'You are my God.'
5. Let your face shine on your servant. Save me in your love.

an object of scorn to my neighbours and of fear to my friends.
My life is in your hands, de - liver me from the hands of those who hate me.
Be strong, let your heart take courage, all who hope in the Lord.

29

## EXTRACT B – vv. 2-4, 17, 25. R/ v. 3

9th Sunday in Ordinary Time (Year A)

*Response:* **Be a rock of re - fuge for me, O Lord.**

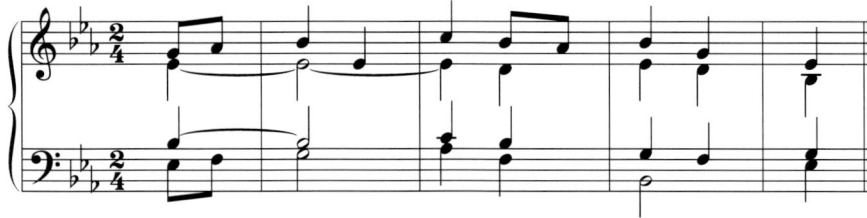

1. In you, O Lord, I take refuge. Let me never be put to shame.
2. Be a rock of re - fuge for me, a mighty stronghold to save me.
3. Let your face shine on your servant. Save me in your love.

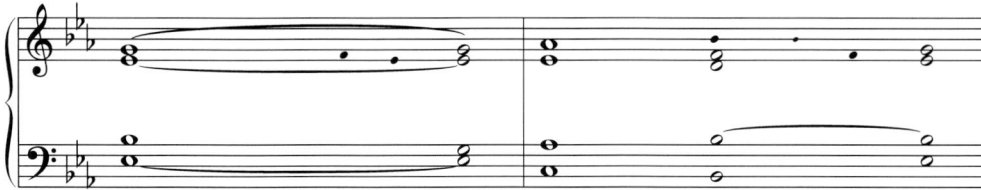

In your justice set me free, hear me and speed - i - ly rescue me.
for you are my rock, my stronghold. For your name's sake, lead me and guide me.
Be strong, let your heart take courage, all who hope in the Lord.

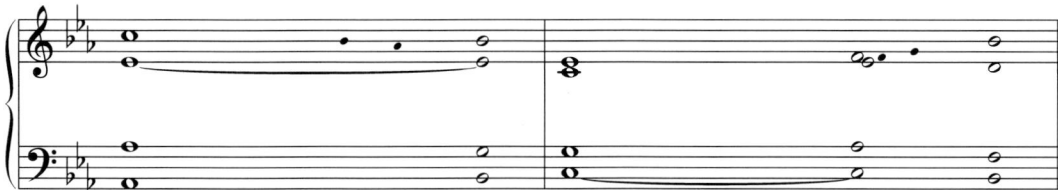

## EXTRACT C – vv. 3-4, 6, 8, 17, 21. R/ v. 6

St Andrew (November 30 – in Scotland)

*Response:* **In - to your hands I com - mend__ my__ spi - rit.**

1. Be a rock of re - fuge for me, a mighty stronghold to save me,
2. Into your hands I com-mend my spirit. It is you who will re-deem me, Lord.
3. Let your face shine on your servant. Save me in your love.

for you are my rock, my stronghold. For your name's sake, lead me and guide me.
As for me, I trust in the Lord, let me be glad and rejoice in the Lord.
* How great is the good-ness, Lord, that you keep for those who fear you.

*\* - This is a correction to the text given in the Lectionary.*

# Psalm 31 (32) – Blessed the sinner whose offence is forgiven

## vv. 1-2, 5, (7,) 11

6th Sunday in Ordinary Time (Year B) - response 1  (v. 7)
11th Sunday in Ordinary Time (Year C) - response 2 (cf v. 5)

*Response 1 (6th Sunday in O.T.):*

You are my re-fuge, O Lord; you fill me with the joy of sal - va - -tion.

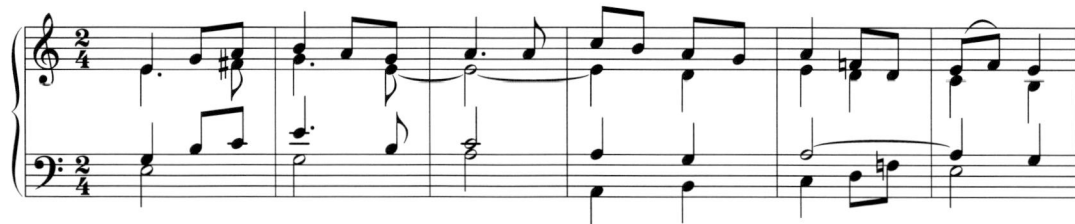

*Response 2 (11th Sunday in O.T.):* For - give, Lord, the guilt of my sin.____

* - *Verse 2a is sung on 11th Sunday of Ordinary Time only*

1. Happy the man whose offence is for-given, whose sin is re- mitted.
2. But now I have acknow - ledged my sins; my guilt I did not hide.
*2a. You are my hiding place, O Lord; [ ]
3. Rejoice, rejoice in the Lord, ex - ult, you just!

*Omit this phrase in verse 2a*

O happy the man to whom the Lord im-putes no guilt,
I said: 'I will con- fess my offence to the Lord.'
* you save me from dis - tress.
O come, ring out your joy,

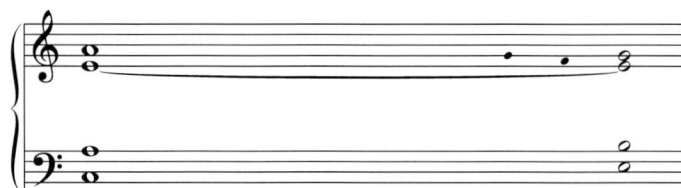

in whose spirit is no guile.
And you, Lord, have forgiven the guilt of my sin.
* You surround me with cries of de-liverance.
all you up - right of heart.

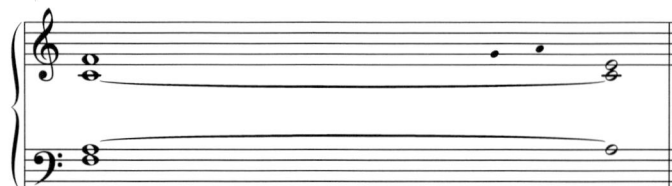

# Psalm 32 (33) – The word of the Lord

## EXTRACT A – vv. 4-5, (6, 9,) 18-20, 22

> 2nd Sunday of Lent (Year A) - response 1 (v. 22)
> 29th Sunday of Ordinary Time (Year B) - response 1 (v. 22)
> Trinity Sunday (Year B) - response 2 (v. 12)

*Response 1 (in Lent and O.T.):* **May your love be up-on us, O Lord, as we place all our hope in you.**

*Response 2 (Trinity Sunday):* **Hap-py the peo-ple the Lord has cho-sen as his own.**

*\* – Verse 1a is sung only on Trinity Sunday*

```
1.    The word of the          Lord  is   faithful    and all his works            to  be trusted.
*1a. By his word the hea  -  vens were   made,        by the breath of his mouth  all  the  stars.
2.    The Lord looks on those who  re - vere him,     on those who hope            in  his   love,
3.    Our soul is waiting       for  the   Lord.      The Lord is our help         and our  shield.
```

```
The Lord loves jus  -  tice  and right    and fills the earth           with his  love.
* He spoke; and they    came  to    be.    He commanded; they sprang  in - to  being.
to rescue their         souls from death,  to keep them a       -       live in famine.
May your love be upon   us,    O   Lord,   as we place all our           hope in  you.
```

33

# PSALM 32 (33)

## EXTRACT B – vv. 1-2, 4-5, 12, 18-20, 22. R/ v. 22

5th Sunday of Easter (Year A)

*Response:* **May your love be up-on us, O Lord, as we place all our hope___ in you.**

1. Ring out your joy to the Lord, O you just; for praise is fitting for loy-al hearts.
2. The word of the Lord is faithful and all his works to be trusted.
3. The Lord looks on those who re-vere him, on those who hope in his love,

Give thanks to the Lord up - on the harp, with a ten-stringed lute sing him songs.
The Lord loves jus - tice and right and fills the earth
to rescue their souls from death, to keep them a - live in famine.

## EXTRACT C – vv. 1-2, 4-5, 12, 18-20, 22. R/ v. 12

19th Sunday of Ordinary Time (Year C)

*Response:* **Hap - py the peo - ple the Lord has cho - sen as___ his own.**

34

# PSALM 32 (33)

1. Ring out your joy to the Lord,   O   you   just;      for praise is fitting for loy - al hearts.
2. The Lord looks on those       who re - vere him,   on those who hope    in   his   love,
3. Our soul is waiting           for   the   Lord.      The Lord is our help   and our shield.

They are happy whose God   is    the   Lord,      the people he has chosen   as   his   own.
to rescue their            souls from death,     to keep them a     -      live   in  famine.
May your love be upon      us,    O   Lord,      as we place all our        hope in   you.

## EXTRACT D – vv. 4-7, 12-13, 20, 22. R/ v. 5

Easter Vigil (after 1st reading, alternative psalm)

*Response:* **The   Lord fills the    earth _ with his   love.**

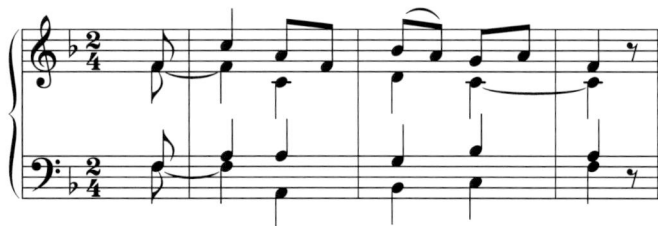

1. The word of the            Lord   is   faithful    and all his works            to   be   trusted.
2. By his word the hea   -   vens were  made,        by the breath of his mouth all   the   stars.
3. They are happy, whose God  is    the   Lord,       the people he has chosen   as   his   own,
4. Our soul is waiting         for   the   Lord.      The Lord is our help        and our  shield.

The Lord loves jus   -   tice   and   right    and fills the earth            with his  love.
He spoke; and they       came   to    be.      He commanded; they sprang  in - to  being.
From the heavens the   Lord looks forth,        he sees all the child     -    ren  of  men.
May your love be upon  us,    O   Lord,         as we place all our          hope in   you.

35

## EXTRACT E – vv. 10-15. R/ v. 12

Pentecost Vigil (after 1st reading)

*Response:* **Hap - py the peo - ple the Lord has cho - sen as___ his own.**

1. He frustrates the designs       of   the nations,     he defeats the plans        of the peoples.
2. They are happy, whose God    is    the Lord,      the people he has chosen as his   own,
3. From the place where he     dwells he   gazes     on all the dwellers          on the   earth,

His own designs shall      stand  for  ever,     the plans of his heart from age   to      age.
From the heavens the       Lord looks forth,    he sees all the child    -   ren  of   men.
he who shapes the hearts   of   them   all      and considers                 all  their deeds.

# Psalm 33 (34) – Taste and see that the Lord is good

## EXTRACT A – vv. 2-9

> 19th Sunday in Ordinary Time (Year B) – response 1 (v. 9)
> Common Psalm 3 for Ordinary Time – response 1
> 4th Sunday of Lent (Year C) – response 1
> SS. Peter & Paul (Day – June 29) – response 2 (v. 5)

*Response 1 (on given Sundays):*  Taste___ and  see  that  the  Lord___ is  good.

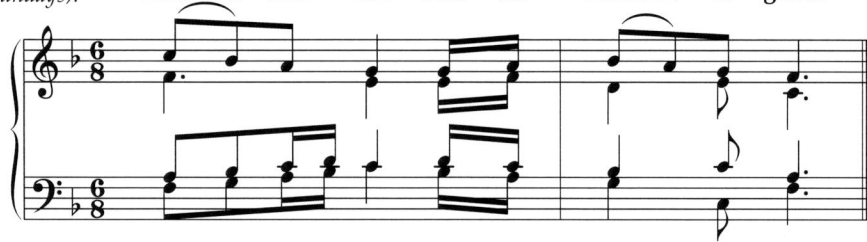

*Response: 2 (SS. Peter & Paul):*  From  all my terr - - ors the  Lord_ set me  free.

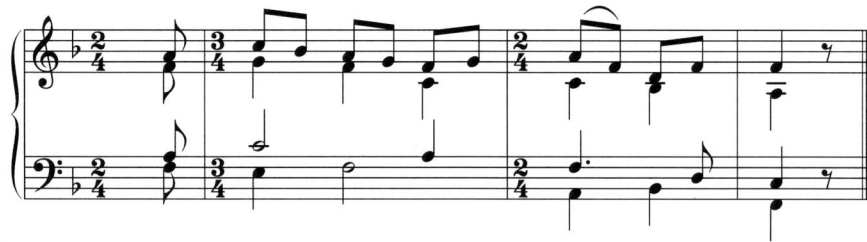

*\* – Verse 4 is omitted on the 4th Sunday of Lent*

1. I will bless the Lord     at   all   times,    his praise always       on   my   lips.
2. Glorify the              Lord with  me.     Together let us         praise his   name.
3. Look towards him     and  be radiant;   let your faces not       be   a - bashed.
*4. The angel of the Lord  is   en - camped   around those who revere  him,  to rescue them.

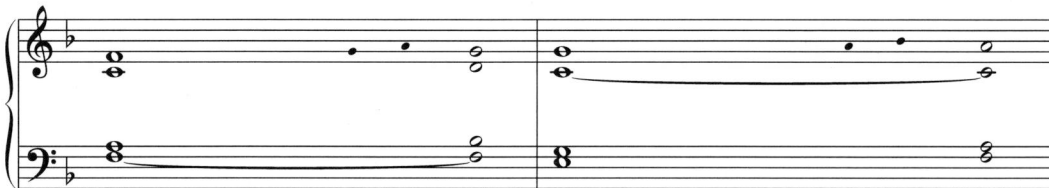

in the Lord my soul shall make  its     boast.    The humble shall hear    and  be glad.
I sought the Lord              and   he  answered me;  from all my terrors he    set me free.
This poor man called;      the  Lord  heard him    and rescued him from all  his  dis-tress.
* Taste and see that the   Lord  is     good.     He is happy who seeks re-fuge in  him.

37

## PSALM 33 (34)

### EXTRACT B – vv. 2-3, 10-15. R/ v. 9

20th Sunday in Ordinary Time (Year B)

*Response:* **Taste___ and see that the Lord___ is good.**

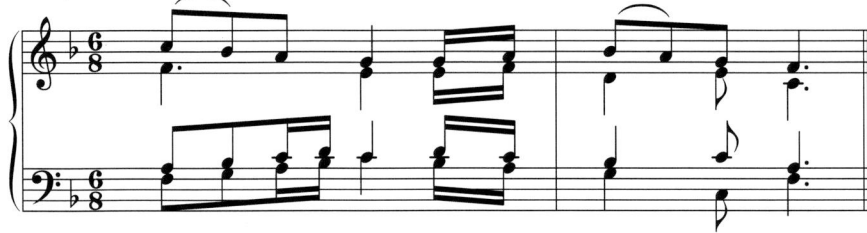

1. I will bless the Lord at all times, his praise always on my lips.
2. Revere the Lord, you his saints. They lack nothing, those who re-vere him
3. Come, child - ren, and hear me that I may teach you the fear of the Lord.
4. Then keep your tongue from evil and your lips from speak - ing de - ceit.

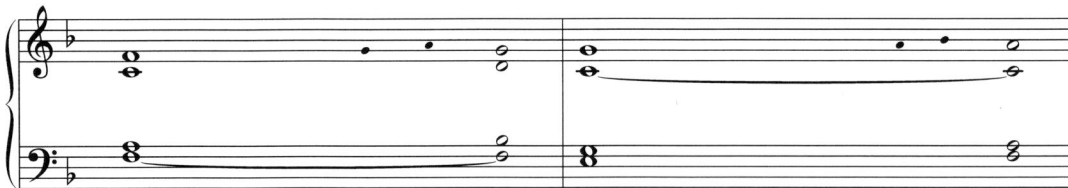

in the Lord my soul shall make its boast. The humble shall hear and be glad.
Strong lions suf- fer want and go hungry but those who seek the Lord lack no blessing.
who is he who longs for life and many days, to enjoy his pros- perity?
Turn aside from evil and do good; seek and strive af - ter peace.

### EXTRACT C – vv. 2-3, 16-23. R/ v. 9

21st Sunday in Ordinary Time (Year B)

*Response 'Taste and see' as above*

1. I will bless the Lord at all times, his praise always on my lips.
2. The Lord turns his face a-gainst the wicked to destroy their remembrance from the earth.
3. They call and the Lord hears and rescues them from all their dis - tress.
4. Many are the trials of the just man but from them all the Lord will rescue him.
5. Ev- il brings death to the wicked; those who hate the good are doomed.

in the Lord my soul shall make its boast. The humble shall hear and be glad.
The Lord turns his eyes to the just and his ears to their ap - peal.
The Lord is close to the bro - ken-hearted; those whose spirit is crushed he will save.
He will keep guard over all his bones, not one of his bones shall be broken.
The Lord ransoms the souls of his servants. Those who hide in him shall not be con-demned.

# PSALM 33 (34)

## EXTRACT D – vv. 2-3, 17-19, 23. R/ v. 7

30th Sunday in Ordinary Time (Year C)

*Response:* **This poor man** **called; the Lord** **heard him.**

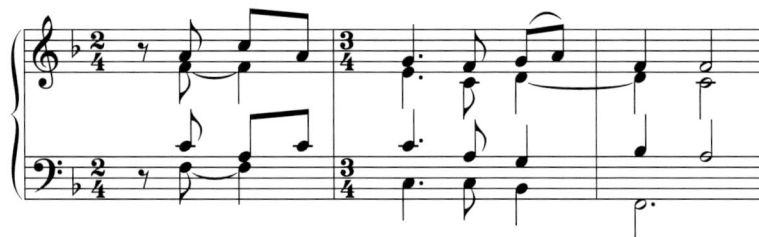

1. I will bless the Lord     at    all    times,     his praise always              on   my   lips.
2. The Lord turns his face a-gainst the   wicked     to destroy their remembrance from the earth.
3. The Lord is close to the    bro - ken-hearted;     those whose spirit is crushed    he   will   save.

in the Lord my soul shall     make its     boast.     The humble shall hear         and   be    glad.
The just call               and   the Lord hears    and rescues them from all      their dis - tress.
The Lord ransoms the souls   of   his   servants.    Those who hide in him shall not   be   con-demned.

# Psalm 39 (40) – You do not ask for sacrifice... but an open ear

EXTRACT A – vv. (2, 4,) 7-10, (11). R/ v. 8, 9

> 2nd Sunday of Ordinary Time (Year A)
> 2nd Sunday of Ordinary Time (Year B)
> Annunciation of the Lord (March 25)

*Response:* **Here I am,     Lord!     I     come to do your     will.**

*\* – Omit on the Annunciation*

*† – On the Annunciation only*

```
*1.  I waited, I waited for                the     Lord     and he stooped down to me; he heard  my     cry.
 2.  You do not ask for sacrifice          and   offerings,   but an o        -        pen    ear.
 3.  In the scroll of the book it          stands  written    that I should do          your   will.
 4.  Your justice I have                   pro - claimed   in the great            as - sembly.
†5.  I have not hidden your justice in   my     heart     but declared your faith    -     ful   help.
```

```
* He put a new song in       -     to   my   mouth,   praise        of   our   God.
You do not ask for holo    -   caust and victim.   Instead,      here am   I.
My God, I delight                in   your   law    in the depth  of   my   heart.
My lips I                    have  not sealed;   you know     it,   O   Lord.
† I have not hidden your love  and  your  truth    from the     great as- sembly.
```

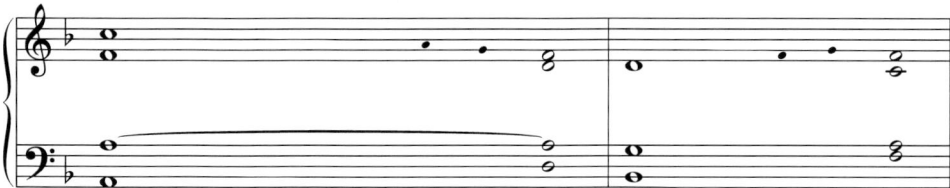

PSALM 39 (40)

## EXTRACT B – vv. 2-4, 18. R/ v. 14

20th Sunday in Ordinary Time (Year C)

*Response:* **Lord,___ come___ to my aid, come___ to my aid!**

1. I waited, I waited for the Lord and he stooped down to me; he heard my cry.

2. He drew me from the dead -ly pit, from the mi - ry clay.
3. He put a new song into my mouth, praise of our God.
4. As for me, wretched and poor, the Lord thinks of me.

He set my feet up -on a rock and made my foot-steps firm.
Many shall see and fear and shall trust in the Lord.
You are my rescu -er, my help, O God, do not de - lay.

41

# Psalm 40 (41) – Blessed be God who cares for the poor

vv. 2-5, 13-14. R/ v. 5

7th Sunday in Ordinary Time (Year B)

*Response:* **Heal my soul for I have sinned a - gainst you.**

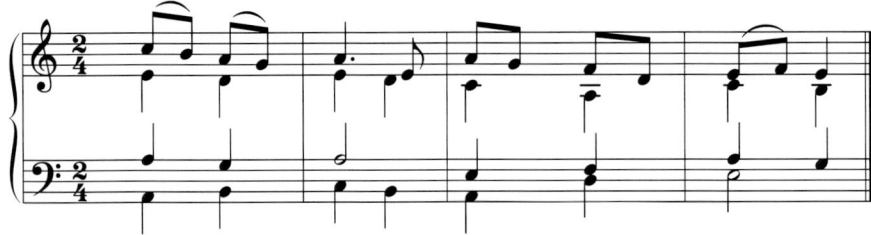

1. Happy the man who considers the poor and the weak.     The Lord will save him in the day        of  evil,
2. The Lord will help him on his            bed of  pain,     he will bring him back from  sick-ness to health.
3. If you uphold me I shall            be un-harmed     and set in your presence for ev   -   er-more.

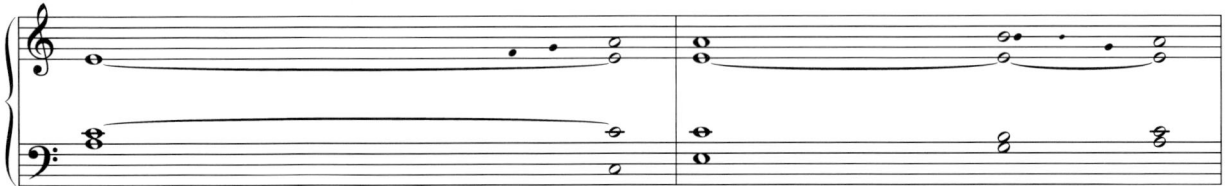

will guard him, give him life, make him happy  in  the  land
As for me, I said: 'Lord, have mer        -        cy  on  me,
Blessed be the Lord, the            God  of  Israel,

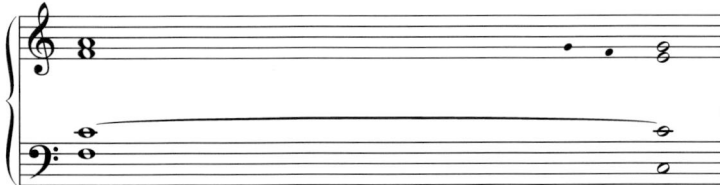

and will not give him up to the will     of   his     foes.
heal my soul for I have            sinned  a - gainst you.'
from age to age. A        -        men.  A - men.

*Blessed be the Lord, the God of Israel, from age to age,*

*Amen. Amen.*

*Psalm 40:14*

*The Conclusion of Book 1*

42

# BOOK 2

PSALMS 41 (42) – 71 (72)

# Psalms 41 & 42 (42 & 43) – Like the deer that yearns for running streams

Ps 41: 3, 5; Ps 42: 3, 4. R/ Ps 41:1

Easter Vigil (after the 7th reading)

*Response:* **Like the deer that yearns for run-ning streams,**

**so my soul is yearn-ing for you, my God.**

*Verses 1, 3 & 4*

1. My soul is thirst - ing for God, the God of my life;
3. O send forth your light and your truth, let these be my guide.
4. And I will come to the al-tar of God, the God of my joy.

when can I en - ter and see the face of God?
Let them bring me to your ho-ly mountain, to the place where you dwell.
My redeemer, I will thank you on the harp, O God, my God.

*Verse 2*

2. These things will I re-member as I pour out my soul: how I would lead the re-joic-ing crowd

into the house of God, amid cries of gladness and thanks-giving, the throng wild with joy.

44

# Psalm 44 (45) – Royal wedding song

vv. 10-12, 16. R/ v. 10

The Assumption of the BVM (Day – August 15)

*Response:* **On your right stands the queen, in gar - ments of gold.**

1. The daughters of kings are a-mong your loved ones. On your right stands the queen in gold of O-phir.
2. So will the king de - sire your beauty: He is your lord, pay hom - age to him.

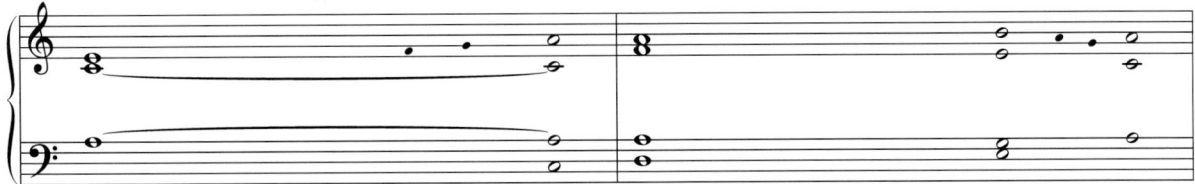

Listen, O daughter, give ear to my words: forget your own people and your fa-ther's house.
They are escorted amid glad-ness and joy; they pass within the palace of the king.

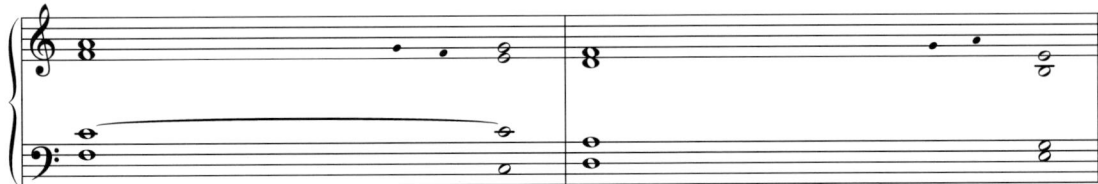

45

# Psalm 45 (46) – God is for us a refuge and strength

vv. 2-3, 5-6, 8-9. R/ v. 5

Dedication of the Lateran Basilica (November 9)

*Response:* **The wa-ters of a riv-er give joy to God's ci--ty, the ho-ly place where the Most_ High_ dwells.**

\* – *This line may be omitted when preceded by the response*

1. God is for us a re - fuge and strength, a helper close at hand, in time of dis - tress:
\*2. The waters of a river give joy to God's city, the holy place where the Most High dwells.
3. The Lord of hosts is with us: the God of Jacob is our stronghold.

so we shall not fear though the earth should rock,
God is within, it can - not be shaken;
Come, consider the works of the Lord,

though the mountains fall into the depths of the sea.
God will help it at the dawning of the day.
the redoubtable deeds he has done on the earth.

# Psalm 46 (47) – All peoples, clap your hands!

## vv. 2-3, 6-9. R/ v. 6

Ascension of the Lord (Vigil & Day)

*Response:* **God goes up with shouts of joy; the Lord goes up with trum--pet blast.**

1. All peo- ples, clap___your hands, cry to God with shouts of joy!
2. God goes up with shouts___ of joy; the Lord goes up with trum - pet blast.
3. God is king of all___ the earth. Sing praise with all your skill.

For the Lord, the Most High, we must fear, great king over all___ the earth.
Sing praise for God, sing praise, sing praise to our king,_ sing praise.
God is king ov - er the nations; God reigns on his ho - - ly throne.

47

# Psalm 49 (50) – The God of gods, the Lord, has spoken

vv. 1, 8, 12-15. R/ v. 23

10th Sunday of Ordinary Time (Year A)

*Response:* **I will show God's sal - va-tion to the up - -right.**

1. The god of gods, the Lord, has spoken and sum-moned the earth, from the rising of the sun to its setting.

*This verse division has been added editorially.*

2. 'I find no fault with your sacrifices, your offerings are al-ways be-fore me.'

3. 'Were I hungry, I would not tell you, for I own the world and all it holds.
4. 'Pay your sacrifice of thanksgiv - ing to God and render him your vo-tive offerings.

Do you think I eat the flesh of bulls, or drink the blood of goats?'
Call on me in the day of dis-tress. I shall free you and you shall honour me.'

# Psalm 50 (51) – Have mercy on me, O God

## EXTRACT A – vv. 3-6, 12-14, 17. R/ v. 3

Ash Wednesday
1st Sunday of Lent (Year A)
Common Psalm 1 for Lent

*Response:* **Have  mer - cy  on  us,  O  Lord,  for  we  have  sinned.**

1. Have mercy on me, God, in your  kindness.    In your compassion blot out  my  of - fence.
2. My offences tru  -  ly  I  know them;  my sin is al  -  ways  be - fore me.
3. A pure heart create for  me,  O  God,    put a steadfast spi  -  rit  with - in me.
4. Give me again the joy  of  your  help;    with a spirit of fer  -  vour  sus - tain me.

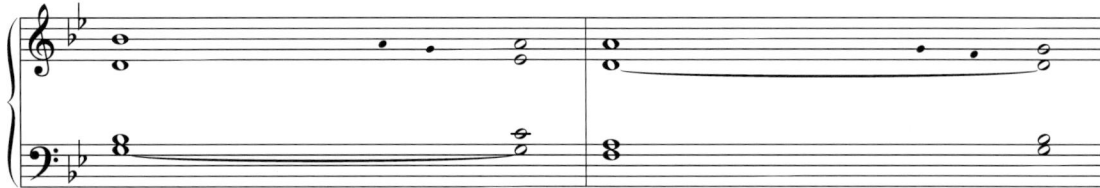

O wash me more and more from  my  guilt    and cleanse me  from  my  sin.
Against you, you alone,  have  I  sinned:    what is evil in your sight  I  have done.
Do not cast me away  from your presence,    nor deprive me of your  ho - ly  spirit.
O Lord, o  -  pen  my  lips    and my mouth shall de - clare your praise.

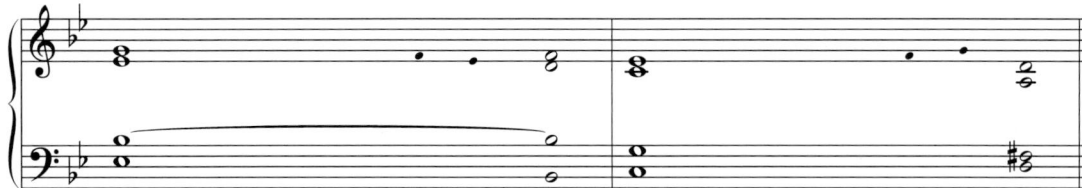

49

# PSALM 50 (51)

## EXTRACT B – vv. 12-15, 18-19. R/ v. 12

Easter Vigil (after 7th reading, alternative)

*Response:* A pure heart cre - ate for me,__ O God.__

1. [                                    ]  put a steadfast spi - rit with - in me.
2. Give me again the joy   of your help;  with a spirit of fer - vour sus - tain me,
3. For in sacrifice you take no de - light, burnt offering from me you would re - fuse,

*omit in verse 1*

Do not cast me away      from your presence,   nor deprive me of your       ho - ly spirit.
that I may teach transgress -ors your  ways   and sinners may re -      turn to you.
my sacrifice, a            con -trite   spirit.  A humbled, contrite heart you will not spurn.

## EXTRACT C – vv. 3-4, 12-13, 14-15 or 17 & 19

5th Sunday of Lent (Year B) – response 1 (v. 12)
24th Sunday in Ordinary Time (Year C) – response 2 (Lk 15:18)

*Response 1 (5th Sunday of Lent):* A pure heart cre - ate for me,__ O God.__

*Response 2 (24th Sunday in O.T.):* I will leave this place and go to my fa - -ther.

*– On 5th Sunday of Lent
† – On 24th Sunday in Ordinary Time

1. Have mercy on me, God, in your kindness. In your compassion blot out my of - fence.
2. A pure heart create for me, O God, put a steadfast spi - rit with - in me.
*3. Give me again the joy of your help; with a spirit of fer - vour sus- tain me,
†3. O Lord, o - pen my lips and my mouth shall de - clare your praise.

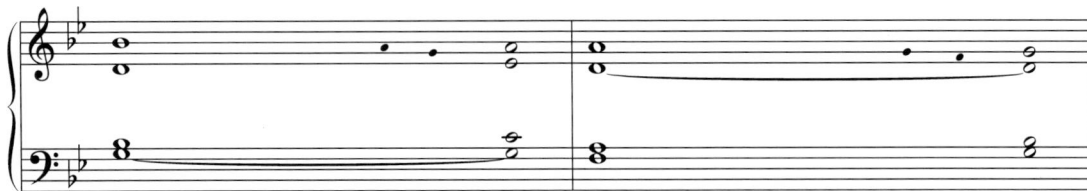

O wash me more and more from my guilt and cleanse me from my sin.
Do not cast me away from your presence, nor deprive me of your ho - ly spirit.
* that I may teach transgress -ors your ways and sinners may re - turn to you.
† My sacrifice, a con - trite spirit. A humbled, contrite heart you will not spurn.

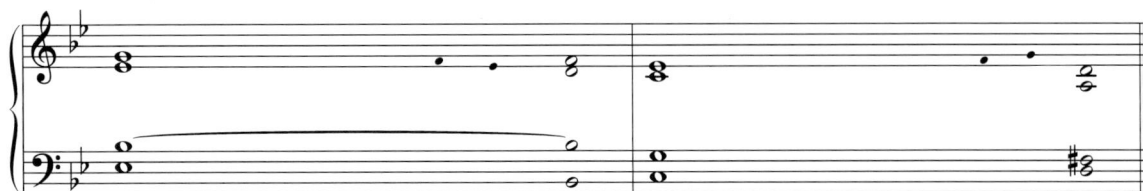

## Psalm 53 (54) – O God, save me by your name

vv. 3-6, 8. R/ v. 6

25th Sunday in Ordinary Time (Year B)

*Response:* **The Lord up - holds my life.**

1. O God, save me by your name; by your power, up -hold my cause.
2. For proud men have ri-sen a - gainst me, ruthless men seek my life.
3. But I have God for my help. The Lord up - holds my life.

O God, hear my prayer; listen to the words of my mouth.
[ ] They have no re - gard for God.
I will sacrifice to you with will-ing heart and praise your name for it is good.

omit in verse 2

51

# Psalm 61 (62) – In God alone is my soul at rest

vv. 2-3, 6-9. R/ v. 6

8th Sunday in Ordinary Time (Year A)

*Response:* **In God a - lone is my soul___ at___ rest.**

*The psalmist continues:*

1.   ...my help comes from him.      He alone is my rock, my stronghold,   my fortress: I stand firm.

2.   In God alone be at rest, my soul;      for my hope comes from him.

He a- lone is my rock, my stronghold,   my fortress: I stand firm.

3.   In God is my safe-ty and glory,      the   rock   of my strength.

Take refuge in God, all you people.   Trust him at all times.   Pour out your hearts be-fore him.

# Psalm 62 (63) — My soul thirsts for God

vv. 2-6, 8-9 or 7-8. R/ v. 2

> 22nd Sunday in Ordinary Time (Year A)
> 32nd Sunday in Ordinary Time (Year A)
> 12th Sunday in Ordinary Time (Year C)
> Common Psalm 4 for Ordinary Time

*Response:* For you my soul is thirst - ing, O Lord___ my___ God.

*\* – Omit on 32nd Sunday in Ordinary Time*
*† – On 32nd Sunday in Ordinary Time only*

|   |   |   |   |   |   |   |   |   |   |
|---|---|---|---|---|---|---|---|---|---|
| 1. | O God, you are my God, for | you | I | long; | for you my | | soul | is | thirsting. |
| 2. | So I gaze on you | in | the | sanctuary | to see your strength | | and | your | glory. |
| 3. | So I will bless you | all | my | life, | in your name I will lift | | up | my | hands. |
| ----- | | | | | | | | | |
| *4. | For you have | been | my | help; | in the shadow of your wings | | I | re - | joice. |
| †4. | On my bed | I | re - member you. | | On you I muse | | through the | | night |

|   |   |   |   |   |   |   |   |
|---|---|---|---|---|---|---|---|
| My body | pines | for | you | like a dry, weary land | with - | out | water. |
| For your love is | bet-ter | than | life, | my lips will | speak | your | praise. |
| My soul shall be filled as | with | a | banquet, | my mouth shall praise | you | with | joy. |
| ----- | | | | | | | |
| * My soul | clings | to | you; | your right hand | holds | me | fast. |
| † for you have | been | my | help; | in the shadow of your wings | I | re - | joice. |

# Psalm 64 (65) – Praise is due to you, O God

## vv. 10-14. R/ Lk 8:8

15th Sunday in Ordinary Time (Year A)

*Response:* **Some___ seed fell in - to rich___ soil and pro - duced___ its crop.**

### Verses 1, 2 & 4

1. You care for the earth, give it water, you fill it with riches.
2. And thus you pro- vide for the earth; you drench its furrows,
4. The hills are gir - ded with joy, the meadows co-vered with flocks,

Your river in hea-ven brims over to pro - vide its grain.
you level it, soften it with showers, you bless its growth.
the valleys are decked with wheat. They shout for joy, yes, they sing.

### Verse 3

3. You crown the year with your goodness. Abundance flows in your steps,

in the pastures of the wilderness it flows.

# Psalm 65 (66) – Cry out with joy to God, all the earth

vv, 1-7, 16, 20. R/ v. 1

> 6th Sunday of Easter (Year A)
> 14th Sunday in Ordinary Time (Year C)
> Common Psalm 2 for Eastertide

*Response:* **Cry out with joy___ to God, all___ the earth.**

*In verse 1, the psalmist continues:*

1. [                              ]  ...O sing to the glory        of his name.
2. 'Before you all the earth shall   bow;   shall sing to you, sing        to your name!'
3. He turned the sea   in - to  dry land,   they passed through the ri-ver  dry - shod.
4. Come and hear, all  who  fear   God.   I will tell what he did        for my   soul:

*omit in verse 1*

O render him glo                ri - ous praise.   Say to God: 'How tremen-dous your  deeds!'
Come and see the            works  of   God,   tremendous his deeds      a - mong  men.
Let our joy then              be    in  him;   he rules for ever          by   his   might.
Blessed be God who did not re - ject   my prayer   nor withhold his          love from   me.

# Psalm 66 (67) – Let all the peoples praise you

vv. 2-3, 5, 6, 8

Solemnity of Mary, Mother of God – response 1 (v. 2)
20th Sunday in Ordinary Time (Year A) – response 2 (v. 4)
6th Sunday of Easter (Year C) – response 2 (v. 4)

*Response 1 (Solemnity of Mary, Mother of God):*

O  God,  be  gra - cious and  bless us.____

*Response 2 (given Sundays):*

Let the    peo-ples praise you, O  God;    let  all  the peo - -ples  praise you.

\* – *Omit first phrase of verse 1 when response 1 is used*

† – *Omit first two phrases of verse 3 on 20th Sunday in Ordinary Time*

*1. O God, be gra    -    cious and bless us    and let your face shed its light  u - pon us.
2.  Let the nations be glad  and  ex - ult    for you rule the        world with   justice.
†3. Let the peoples praise  you,  O    God;    let all the            peo - ples praise you.

So will your ways be known up - on  earth    and all nations learn your  sa - ving   help.
With fairness you            rule the peoples,    you guide the na    -    tions on    earth.
(3.) May God still give        us  his blessing    till the ends of the        earth re - vere him.

56

# Psalm 67 (68) – The journey of God's people: a thanksgiving

vv. 4-7, 10-11. R/ cf v. 11

22nd Sunday in Ordinary Time (Year C)

*Response:* **In your good-ness, O___ God, you pre - pared___ a home___ for the poor.**

1. The just shall rejoice at the pre-sence of God,
2. Father of the orphan, defender of the widow,
3. You poured down, O God, a ge - ne - rous rain:

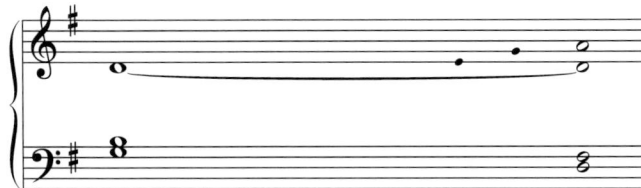

they shall exult and dance___ for joy.
such is God in his ho - - ly place.
when your people were starved you gave them new life.

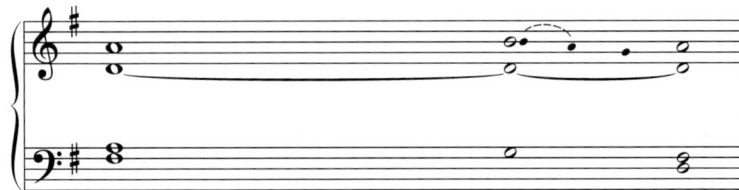

O sing to the Lord, make music to his name; rejoice in the Lord, exult at his presence.
God gives the lonely a home to live in; he leads the prisoners forth in - to freedom.
It was there that your people found a home, prepared in your goodness, O God, for the poor.

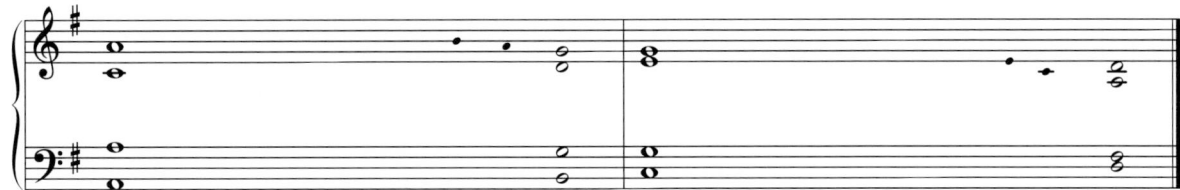

57

# Psalm 68 (69) – Save me, O God!

EXCERPT A – vv. 8-10, 14, 17, 33-35. R/ v. 14

12th Sunday in Ordinary Time (Year A)

*Response:* **In your great love, ans - wer me, O God.**

1. It is for you that I    suf - fer taunts,    that shame    cov - ers my face,
2. This is my    prayer to you,    my    prayer for your favour.
3. The poor when they see it will be glad    and God-seeking hearts will re - vive;

that I have become a stranger to my brothers,    an alien to my    mo-ther's sons.
In your great love, answer    me O    God,    with your help that    ne - ver fails:
for the Lord listens    to the needy    and does not spurn his servants in their chains.

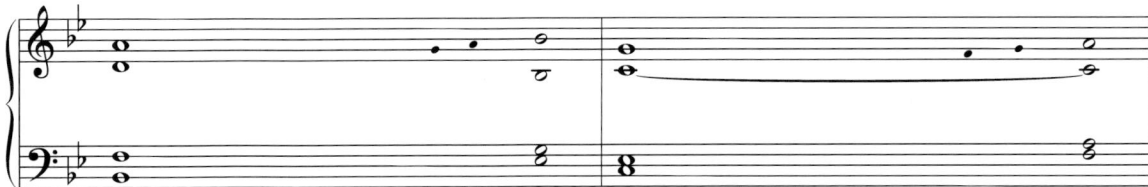

I burn with zeal    for your house    and taunts against you fall on    me.
Lord, answer, for your    love is kind;    in your compassion,    turn to-wards me.
Let the heavens and the earth give him praise,    the sea and all its    liv-ing creatures.

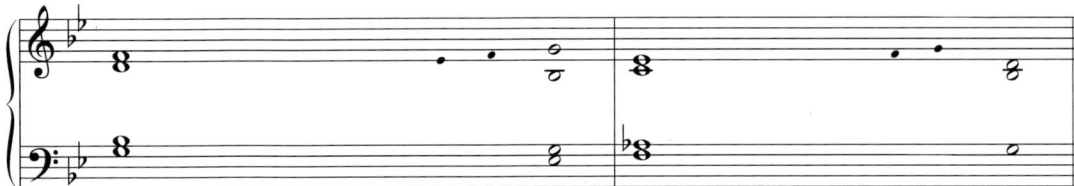

EXCERPT B – vv. 14,17, 30-31, 33-34, 36-37. R/ v. 33

15th Sunday in Ordinary Time (Year C)

*Response:* **Seek the Lord,      you who are poor, and your      hearts _ will re - vive.**

1. This is my prayer to you,      my   prayer for your favour.

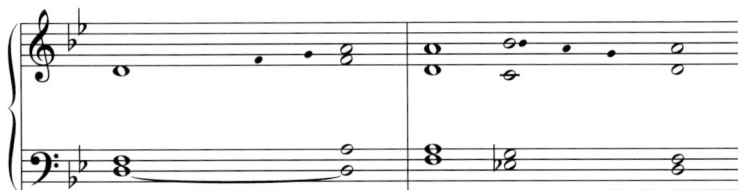

In your great love, answer me O God,      with your help that ne-ver fails:

Lord, answer, for your love is kind;      in your compassion, turn to-wards me.

2. As for me in my pover   -   ty  and pain      let your help, O God,      lift me  up.
3. The poor when they see it  will  be  glad      and God-seeking hearts will re - vive;
4. For God will bring           help  to  Zion      and rebuild the cit    -    ies  of Judah.

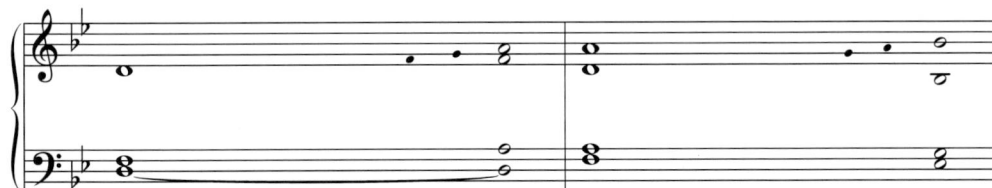

I will praise God's name  with  a   song;      I will glorify him              with  thanks - giving.
for the Lord listens           to  the needy      and does not spurn his servants   in     their      chains.
The sons of his servants shall  in- herit it;      those who love his              name  shall  dwell there.

# Psalm 70 (71) – In you, O Lord, I take refuge

vv. 1-6, 15, 17

4th Sunday in Ordinary Time (Year C) – response 1 (v. 15)
Nativity of St John the Baptist (Vigil – June 23) – response 2 (v. 6)

*Response 1 (4th Sunday in O.T.):*  **My lips will tell__ of your help.**

*Response 2 (June 23):*  **From my mo-ther's womb you have been my help.**

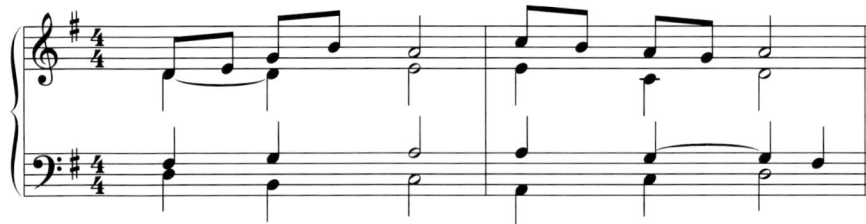

1. In you, O Lord,        I take refuge;        let me never be    put    to    shame.
2. Be a rock where I      can take refuge,      a mighty strong - hold   to   save me;
3. It is you, O Lord, who are my   hope,        my trust, O Lord, since my   youth.
4. My lips will tell           of your justice    and day by day    of your   help.

In your justice res      -      cue me, free me:    pay heed to                    me  and save me.
for you are my                    rock, my stronghold.   Free me from the hand          of   the  wicked.
On you I have leaned          from my    birth,       from my mother's womb you have been  my    help.
O God, you have taught me from my    youth       and I proclaim your                won-ders   still.

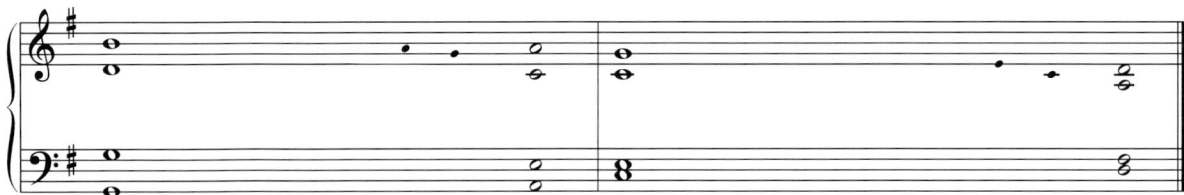

60

# Psalm 71 (72) – O God, give your judgment to the king

EXTRACT A – vv. 1-2, 7-8, 10-13. R/ cf v. 11

The Epiphany of the Lord (Vigil and Day)

*Response:* **All na - -tions shall fall pro - -strate be - fore___ you, O Lord.**

1. O God, give your judgement                               to    the    king,
2. In his days jus                           -             tice  shall flourish
3. The kings of Tarsh- ish and the sea coasts shall  pay   him   tribute.
4. For he shall save the poor                         when  they    cry

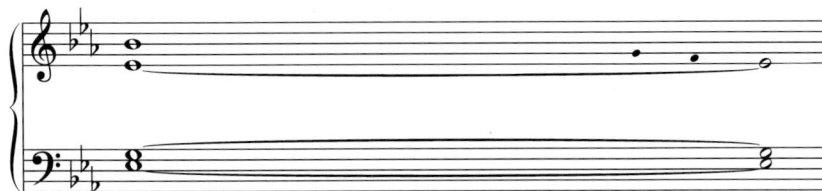

to a king's                                   son   your   justice,
and peace till                              the   moon    fails.
The kings of Sheba and Seba shall bring  him     gifts.
and the needy                             who   are   helpless.

that he may judge your peo -ple  in    justice    and your poor          in    right judgement.
He shall rule from              sea  to    sea,   from the Great River  to   earth's  bounds.
Before him all kings         shall fall prostrate,  all na        -      tions  shall  serve him.
He will have pity            on   the   weak      and save the lives   of    the    poor.

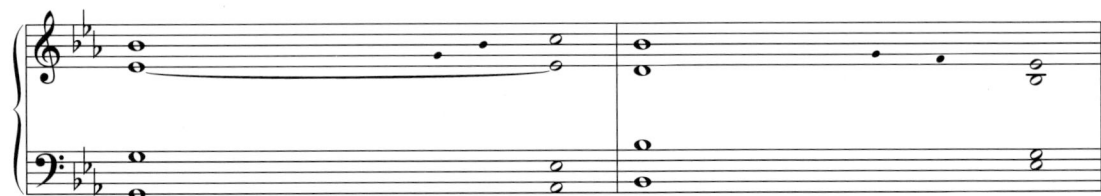

# PSALM 71 (72)

## EXTRACT B – vv. 1-2, 7-8, 12-13, 17. R/ cf v. 7

2nd Sunday of Advent (Year A)

*Response:* **In his days jus-tice shall flou-rish and peace till the moon___ fails.**

1. O God, give your judgement to the king, to a king's son your justice,
2. In his days jus - tice shall flourish and peace till the moon fails.
3. For he shall save the poor when they cry and the needy who are helpless.
4. May his name be blessed for ever and endure like the sun.

that he may judge your peo - ple in justice and your poor in right judgement.
He shall rule from sea to sea, from the Great River to earth's bounds.
He will have pity on the weak and save the lives of the poor.
Every tribe shall be blessed in him, all nations bless his name.

*Blessed be the Lord, God of Israel,*

*who alone works wonders,*

*ever blessed his glorious name.*

*Let his glory fill the earth.*

*Amen! Amen!*

*Psalm 71: 18-19*
*The Conclusion of Book 2*

# BOOK 3

PSALMS 72 (73) – 88 (89)

# Psalm 77 (78) – The lessons of history

EXTRACT A – vv. 3-4, 23-25, 54. R/ v. 24

18th Sunday in Ordinary Time (Year B)

*Response:* **The Lord gave them bread from___ hea - ven.**

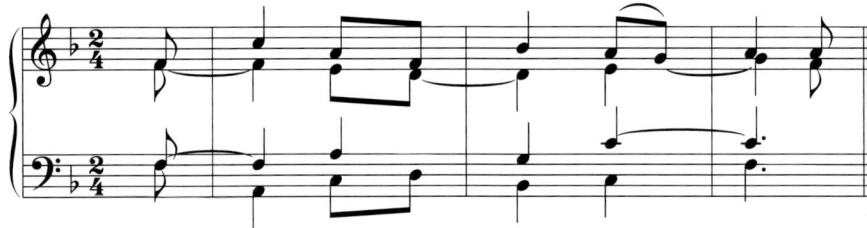

1. The things we have heard and un - der-stood, the things our fa - thers have told us,
2. He commanded the clouds a - bove and opened the gates of heaven.
3. Mere men ate the bread of angels. He sent them abun-dance of food.

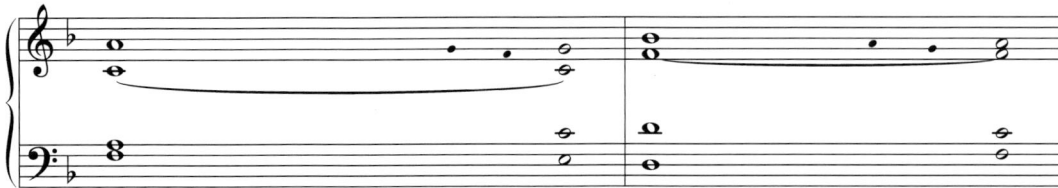

we will tell to the next ge - ne - ration: the glories of the Lord and his might.
He rained down manna for their food, and gave them bread from heaven.
He brought them to his ho - ly land, to the mountain which his right hand had won.

## EXTRACT B – vv. 1-2, 34-38. R/ v. 7

Exaltation of the Holy Cross (September 14)

*Response:* **Ne-ver for-get the deeds _ of the Lord.**

1. Give heed, my people, to my teaching; turn your ear to the words of my mouth.
2. When he slew them, then they would seek him, return and seek him in earnest.
3. But the words they spoke were mere flattery; they lied to him with their lips.
4. Yet he who is full of com - passion forgave their sin and spared them.

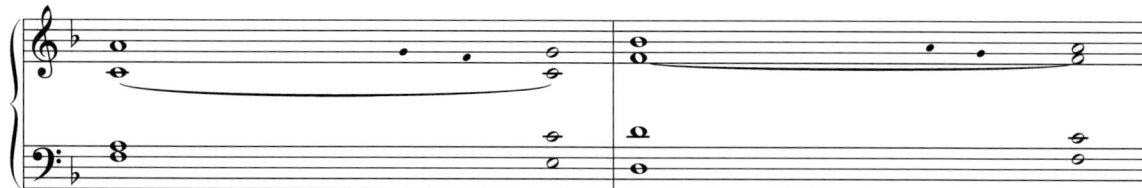

I will open my mouth in a parable and reveal hidden lessons of the past.
They would remember that God was their rock, God the Most High their re - deemer.
For their hearts were not tru - ly with him; they were not faithful to his covenant.
So often he held back his anger, when he might have stirred up his rage.

# Psalm 79 (80) – The vine of Israel

EXTRACT A – vv. 2-3, 15-16, 18-19. R/ v.4

1st Sunday of Advent (Year B)
4th Sunday of Advent (Year C)

*Response:* **God of hosts, bring us back; let your face shine on us and we shall be saved.**

1. O shepherd of Is - ra - el, hear us, shine forth from your che - ru - bim throne.
2. God of hosts, turn again, we im - plore, look down from hea - ven and see.
3. May your hand be on the man you have chosen, the man you have gi - ven your strength.

O Lord, rouse up your might. O Lord, come to our help.
Visit this vine and pro - tect it, the vine your right hand has planted.
And we shall never forsake you a - gain: give us life that we may call up - on your name.

EXTRACT B – vv. 9, 12-16, 19-20. R/ Is 5:7

27th Sunday in Ordinary Time (Year A)

*Response:* **The vine-yard of the Lord is the house of Is - ra - el.**

66

1. You brought a vine     out of Egypt; to plant it you drove     out the nations.
2. Then why have you broken down its walls? It is plucked by all     who pass   by.
3. God of hosts, turn again,   we im-plore, look down from hea - ven and   see.
4. And we shall never forsake you a - gain: give us life that we may call up -on your name.

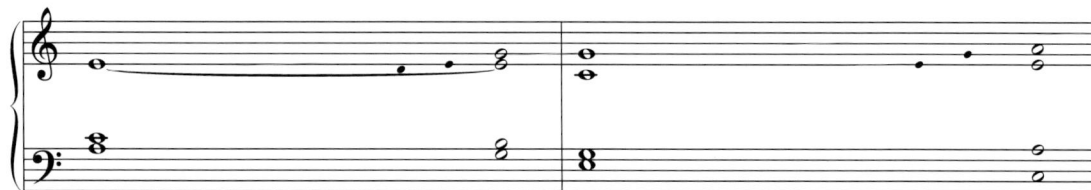

It stretched out its branches   to   the   sea, to the Great River it     stretched out its shoots.
It is ravaged by the boar     of   the forest, devoured by the     beasts   of   the   field.
Visit this vine     and pro-tect it, the vine your     right   hand has planted.
God of hosts,     bring us   back; let your face shine on us and   we    shall be   saved.

## Psalm 80 (81) – Listen, my people!

vv. 3-8, 10-11. R/ v. 2

9th Sunday in Ordinary Time (Year B)

*Response:* **Ring out your joy to     God— our strength.**

1. Raise a song and     sound the timbrel, the sweet-sounding harp and the   lute,
2. For this is Is -     ra - el's   law, a command of the     God of Jacob.
3. A voice I did not know   said   to    me: 'I freed your shoulder     from the burden;
4. 'Let there be no foreign god a - mong you, no worship of an a -     li - en   god.

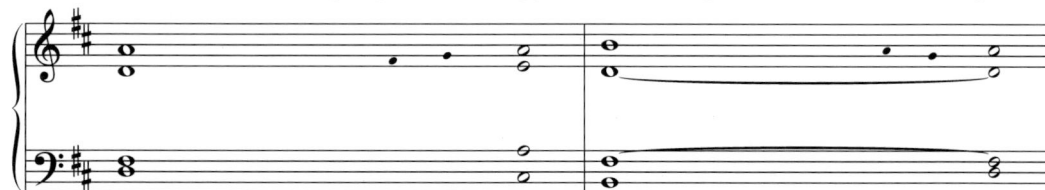

blow the trumpet     at    the new moon, when the moon is full,     on our   feast.
He imposed it as a     rule   on    Joseph, when he went out against the land of    Egypt.
your hands were freed from the     load. You called in distress     and   I   saved you.'
I am the     Lord your    God, who brought you from the     land of    Egypt.'

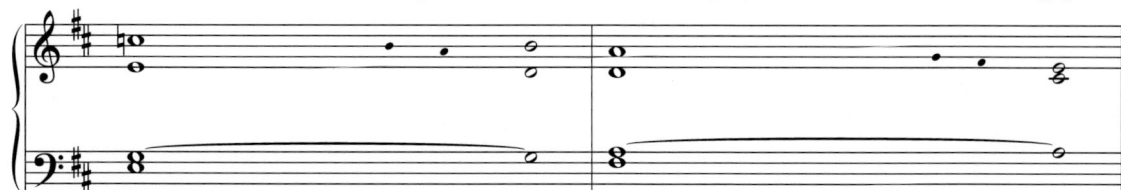

# Psalm 83 (84) – How lovely is your dwelling-place

vv. 2-3, 5-6, 9-10. R/ v. 5

> Holy Family (Year C) – response 1 (v. 5)
> Anniversary of Dedication of a Church – response 2 (v. 2) or 3 (Rev 21:3)

*Response 1 (for Holy Family):* **They are hap-py who dwell in your house, O Lord.**

*Response 2 (for Anniversary of Dedication):* **How love-ly is your dwel-ling place, Lord, God of hosts.**

*Response 3 (for Anniversary of Dedication – alternative):* **Here God lives a-mong men.**

*This line is optional when preceded by Response 2*

1. [How love- ly is your dwelling place, Lord, God of hosts.]

My soul is long-ing and yearning, is yearning for the courts of the Lord.

My heart and my soul ring out their joy to God, the liv-ing God.

68

2. They are happy who dwell  in  your house,      for ever     sing-ing your praise.
3. O Lord, God of hosts,       hear  my  prayer,    give ear, O God       of   Jacob.

They are happy, whose strength  is   in   you;      they walk with ever-grow-ing strength.
Turn your eyes, O                  God, our shield,    look on the face of   your  an - ointed.

## Psalm 84 (85) – Bring us back, O God, our Saviour!

vv. 9-14. R/ v. 8

19th Sunday in Ordinary Time (Year A)
2nd Sunday of Advent (Year B)
15th Sunday in Ordinary Time (Year B)
Common Psalm 2 for Advent

*Response:* **Let us    see,___  O Lord,___ your    mer -   cy___    and    give us your sa - ving    help.**

1. I will hear what the Lord God  has   to    say,     a voice that speaks of peace, peace  for  his people.
2. Mercy and faithful   -   ness have  met,     justice and peace              have em-braced.
3. The Lord will            make  us  prosper   and our earth shall          yield its  fruit.

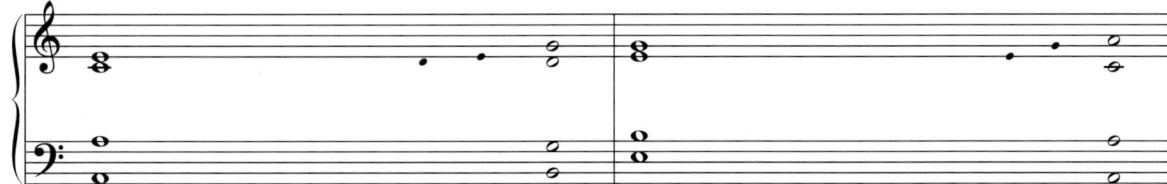

His help is near for        those who fear him     and his glory will dwell  in   our   land.
Faithfulness shall spring from the   earth     and justice look   down___ from heaven.
Justice shall              march be - fore him   and peace shall     fol - low his   steps.

69

# Psalm 85 (86) – Fear of the Lord

vv. 5-6, 9-10, 15-16. R/ v. 5

16th Sunday in Ordinary Time (Year A)

*Response:* O Lord, you are good__ and for - giv - -ing.

*For verse 1 the psalmist continues:*

1. ...full of love to            all who   call.   [                   ]
2. All the nations shall come and a - dore you   and glorify your name, O Lord:
3. But you, God of mercy   and com-passion,   slow to        ang - er,   O

*omit in verse 1*

Give heed, O Lord,       to   my prayer   and attend to the sound of my voice.
for you are great and do marvel-lous deeds,   you who a - lone__ are God.
abounding in       love and truth,   turn and take   pi - ty on  me.

# Psalm 88 (89) – I will sing for ever of your love, O Lord

EXTRACT A – vv. 4-5, 16-17, 27, 29. R/ v. 2.

The Nativity of the Lord (Vigil Mass)

*Response:* I will sing__ for e - ver of your love,__ O Lord.

1. 'I have made a covenant          with my chosen one; I have sworn to Da  -  vid my  servant:
2. Happy the people who acclaim such  a      king,      who walk, O Lord, in the light  of  your    face,
3. He will say to me: 'You          are  my   father,    my God, the                rock who saves me.'

I will establish your dynas - ty  for   ever       and set up your throne            through all  ages.'
who find their joy every day  in  your  name,     who make your justice the source   of    their bliss.
I will keep my love          for  him  always;    for him my covenant            shall   en - dure.

## EXTRACT B – vv. 2-3, 16-19. R/ v. 2

13th Sunday in Ordinary Time (Year A)

*Response:* **I will    sing__  for  e - ver of your    love,__  O Lord.**

1. [                              ]
2. Happy the people who acclaim        such  a    king,
3. For it is you, O Lord, who are the glory  of  their strength;

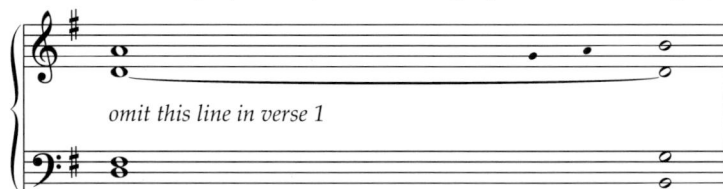

*omit this line in verse 1*

Through all ages my mouth will pro-claim your truth.
who walk, O Lord, in the light          of   your face,
it is by your favour that our might      is    ex - alted:

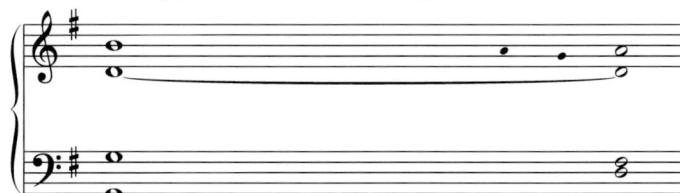

Of this I am sure, that your love lasts  for  ever,     that your truth is firmly established  as  the  heavens.
who find their joy every day       in  your name,     who make your justice the source    of  their   bliss.
for our ruler is in the keeping      of   the Lord;    our king in the keeping of the Holy  One  of    Israel.

71

EXTRACT C – vv. 2-5, 27, 29. R/ v. 2

> 4th Sunday of Advent (Year B) – response 1 (v. 2)
> St Joseph (March 19) – response 2 (v. 37)

*Response 1 (for 4th Sunday of Advent):*   I will sing___ for e - ver of your love,___ O Lord.

*Response 2 (for St Joseph):*   His dy - nas - ty shall last_____ for ev - - er.

*This first line may be omitted on the 4th Sunday of Advent*
1. [I will sing for ever of your love, O    Lord.]
2. 'I have made a covenant    with my chosen one;
3. He will say to me: 'You    are my    father,

Through all ages my mouth will pro-claim your    truth.
I have sworn to Da    -    vid my    servant:
my God, the    rock who saves me.'

Of this I am sure, that your love lasts for    ever,
I will establish your dynas    -    ty for    ever
I will keep my love    for him always;

that your truth is firmly established    as    the heavens.
and set up your throne    through all    ages.'
for him my covenant    shall en - dure.

*Blessed be the Lord for ever.*
*Amen, Amen!*

*Psalm 88: 53*
*The Conclusion of Book 3*

# BOOK 4

PSALMS 89 (90) – 105 (106)

# Psalm 89 (90) – The brevity of life

### EXTRACT A – vv. 12-17. R/ v. 14

28th Sunday in Ordinary Time (Year B)

*Response:* **Fill us with your love that we may re - joice.**

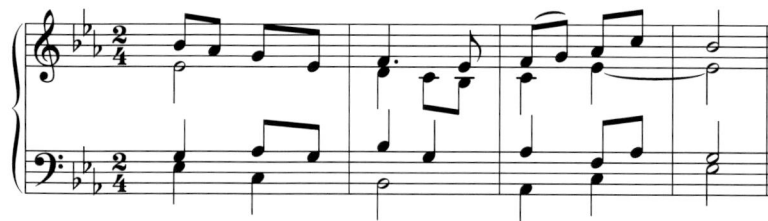

1. Make us know the shortness of our life    that we may gain wis - dom of heart.
2. In the morning, fill us    with your love;    we shall exult and rejoice all our days.
3. Show forth your work    to your servants;    let your glory shine    on their children.

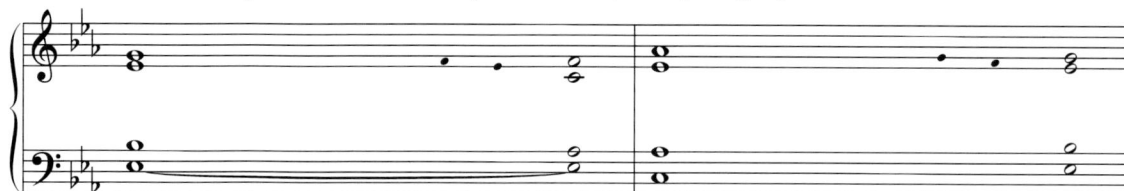

Lord, relent! Is your an - ger for ever?    Show pity    to your servants.
Give us joy to balance    our af - fliction    for the years when we    knew mis - fortune.
Let the favour of the Lord be up - on us:    give suc - cess to the work of our hands.

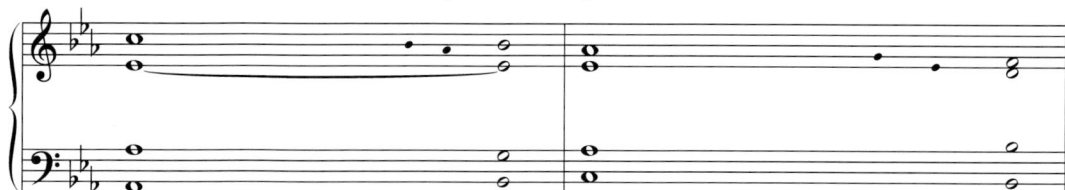

### EXTRACT B – vv. 3-6, 12-14, 17. R/ v. 1

18th Sunday in Ordinary Time (Year C)
23rd Sunday in Ordinary Time (Year C)

*Response:* **O Lord, you have been our re - -fuge from one ge-ne - ra-tion to the next.**

1. You turn men back    in - to dust    and say: 'Go back,    sons of men.'
2. You sweep men away    like a dream,    like grass which springs up in the morning.
3. Make us know the shortness of our life    that we may gain wis - dom of heart.
4. In the morning, fill us    with your love;    we shall exult and rejoice    all our days.

To your eyes a thousand years are like yesterday, come and gone,
In the morning it springs up and flowers:
Lord, relent! Is your an - ger for ever?
Let the favour of the Lord be up - on us:

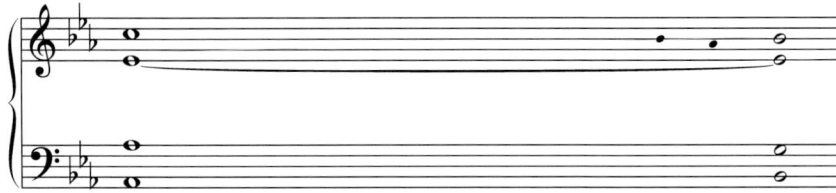

no more than a watch in the night.
by evening it with - ers and fades.
Show pity to your servants.
give success to the work of our hands.

## Psalm 90 (91) – He who dwells in the shelter of the Most High

vv. 1-2, 10-15. R/ v. 15

1st Sunday of Lent (Year C)
Common Psalm 2 for Lent

*Response:* **Be with me, O Lord, in my_ dis - tress.**

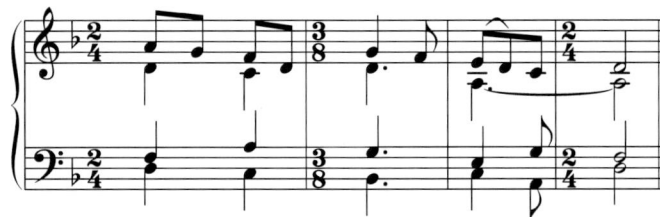

1. He who dwells in the shelter of the Most High and abides in the shade of the Al-mighty
2. Upon you no ev - il shall fall, no plague approach where you dwell.
3. They shall bear you up - on their hands lest you strike your foot a-gainst a stone.
4. His love he set on me, so I will rescue him; protect him for he knows my name.

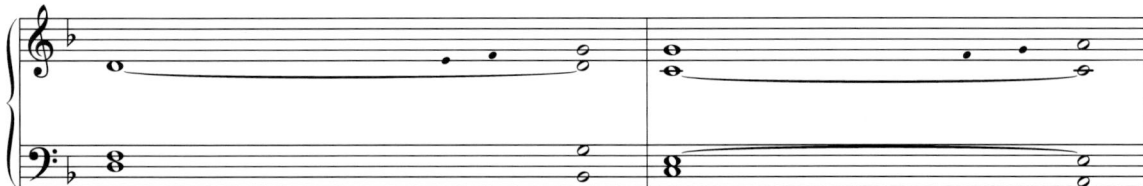

says to the Lord: 'My re - fuge, my stronghold, my God in whom I trust!'
For you has he comman - ded his angels, to keep you in all your ways.
On the lion and the viper you will tread and trample the young lion and the dragon.
When he calls I shall answer: 'I am with you.' I will save him in distress and give him glory.

# Psalm 91 (92) – It is good to give thanks to the Lord

vv. 2-3, 13-16. R/ cf v. 2

11th Sunday in Ordinary Time (Year B)
8th Sunday in Ordinary Time (Year C)

*Response:* **It is good to give you thanks,__ O__ Lord.**

**Verses 1 & 3**

1. It is good to give thanks to the Lord,    to make music to your name,   O Most High,
3. Planted in the    house of the Lord    they will flourish in the courts of our   God,

[                                                    ]
still bearing fruit when they are old,    still full of sap, still green,

*omit this line in verse 1*

to proclaim your love   in   the morning    and your truth in the watches of the  night.
to proclaim that the   Lord  is    just.    In him, my rock, there        is  no  wrong.

**Verse 2**

2. The just will flourish like the palm tree    and grow like a Le-ba-non cedar.

76

# Psalm 92 (93) – Praise God, king of the world!

vv. 1-2, 5. R/ v. 1

Christ the King (Year B)

*Response:* **The Lord is king, with ma-jes-ty en - robed.**

*The psalmist continues:*

1. ...the Lord has robed him-self with might,   he has girded him-self with power.

2. The world you made firm, not to be moved;   your throne has stood firm  from  of old.
3. Truly your decrees are   to be trusted.   Holiness is fitting to your   house, O Lord,

From all eternity, O Lord, you  are.
until the   end  of time.

77

# Psalm 94 (95) — O that today you would listen to his voice

vv. 1-2, 6-9. R/ v. 8

> 3rd Sunday of Lent (Year A)
> 23rd Sunday in Ordinary Time (Year A)
> 4th Sunday in Ordinary Time (Year B)
> 18th Sunday in Ordinary Time (Year C - alternative)
> 27th Sunday in Ordinary Time (Year C)
> Common Psalm 5 for Ordinary Time

*Response:* O that to - day you would lis-ten to his voice! Har - - den not your hearts.

1. Come, ring out our joy          to the Lord;     hail the                    rock who saves us.
2. Come in; let us bow          and bend  low;     let us kneel before the     God who made us
3. O that today you would listen to  his voice!     'Harden not your hearts as  at  Me - ribah

Let us come before him,  giv-ing thanks,      [                                              ]
for he                    is our  God     and we the people who belong to his pasture,
as on that day at Massah  in  the  desert     when your fathers put me        to the  test;

*omit in verse 1*

with songs let us                 hail the  Lord.
the flock that is led             by  his  hand.
when they tried me, though they saw my work.'

# Psalm 95 (96) – Sing a new song to the Lord

EXTRACT A – vv. 1-3, 11-13. R/ Lk 2:11

The Nativity of the Lord: Mass during the Night

*Response:* **To - day a sa-viour has been born__ to us; he is Christ the__ Lord.**

1. O sing a new song to the Lord, sing to the Lord all the earth, O sing to the Lord, bless__ his name.
2. Proclaim his help day by day, tell among the na - tions his glory and his wonders a-mong all the peoples.

3. Let the heavens rejoice and earth be glad, let the sea and all within it thun - der praise,

let the land and all it bears re-joice, all the trees of the wood shout for joy

at the presence of the Lord for he comes, he comes to rule_the earth.

4. With jus- tice he will rule the world, he will judge the peoples with_his truth.

# PSALM 95 (96)

### EXTRACT B – vv. 1, 3-5, 7-10. R/ v. 2

29th Sunday in Ordinary Time (Year A)

*Response:* **Give__ the Lord        glo - - ry and power.**

1.  O sing a new song          to the Lord,    sing to the Lord all____ the earth,
2.  The Lord is great and wor-thy of   praise,   to be feared a - bove____ all   gods;
3.  Give the Lord, you fami - lies of peoples,   give the Lord      glo - ry and power,
4.  Worship the Lord          in his temple.    O earth,      trem - ble be- fore him.

tell among the na   -   tions his glory    and his wonders a - mong all the peoples.
the gods of the hea   -   thens are naught.    It was the Lord who made__ the heavens.
give the Lord the glory    of his name.    Bring an offering and en - ter his courts.
Proclaim to the nations: 'God is   king.'    He will judge the      peo - ples in fairness.

### EXTRACT C – vv. 1-3, 7-10. R/ v. 3

2nd Sunday in Ordinary Time (Year C)

*Response:* **Pro - claim the    won - ders of the    Lord a - mong__ all the    peo - ples.**

80

1. O sing a new song        to the Lord,     sing to the Lord   all____   the   earth,
2. Proclaim his help       day by   day,      tell among the    na‑tions his    glory
3. Give the Lord, you fami‑lies of peoples,   give the Lord     glo ‑ ry   and power,
4. Worship the Lord      in his temple.    O earth,       trem ‑ ble   be‑fore him.

[                  ]    O sing to the Lord,       bless__   his   name.
[                  ]    and his wonders among   all__    the peoples.
[                  ]    give the Lord the glory    of__    his   name.
Proclaim to the nations: 'God is king.'    He will judge the       peo‑ples in fairness.

*verse 4 only*

## Psalm 96 (97) – The Lord is king, let earth rejoice

EXTRACT A –vv. 1, 6, 11-12

The Nativity of the Lord (Mass at Dawn)

*Response:* **This   day new light will   shine up-on the    earth:    the    Lord   is    born for__   us.**

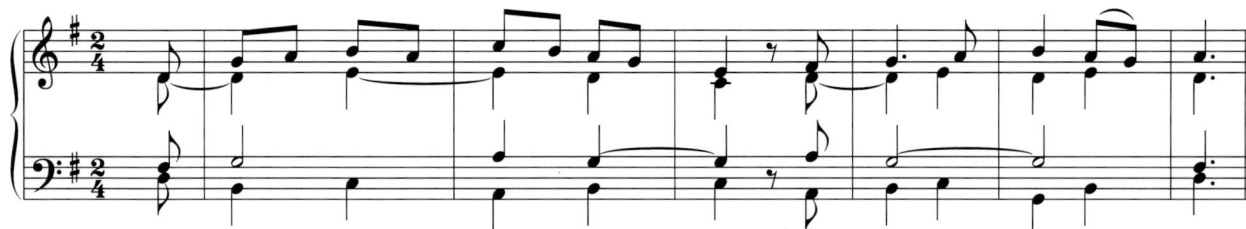

1. The Lord is king, let earth re‑joice,    the many coast ‑ lands be glad.
2. Light shines forth     for the just     and joy for the up‑right of heart.

The skies pro ‑ claim his justice;     all peoples       see his glory.
Rejoice, you just,   in   the Lord;    give glo‑ry to his ho ‑ ly   name.

# PSALM 96 (97)

## EXTRACT B – vv. 1-2, 6-7, 9. R/ vv. 1, 9

7th Sunday of Easter (Year C)

*Response:* **The   Lord is       king, most   high a-bove all the    earth.**

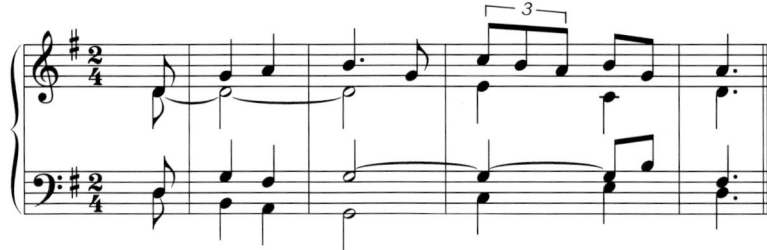

1.   The Lord is king, let   earth re - joice,      let all the coast - lands be  glad.      His throne is jus - tice  and  right.
2.   The skies pro     -     claim his justice;      all peoples            see  his glory.      All you spirits,      wor-ship  him.
3.   For you indeed            are  the Lord       most high above     all   the earth      exalted far a  -  bove all  spirits.

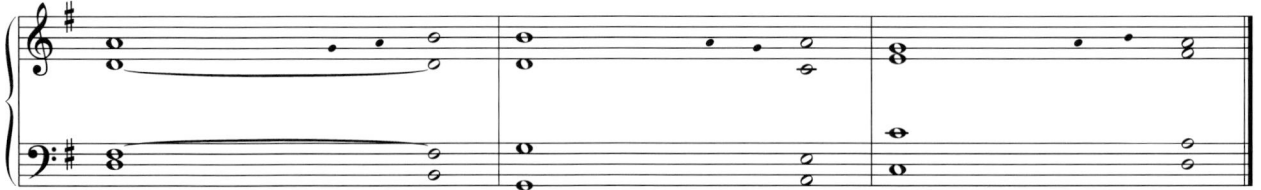

## EXTRACT C – vv. 1-2, 5-6, 9. R/ vv. 1, 9

Transfiguration of the Lord (August 6)

*Response: 'The Lord is king...', as above*

1. .  The Lord is king, let earth  re- joice,     let all the coast  - lands be  glad.
2.   The mountains         melt like wax      before the Lord of  all  the earth.
3.   For you indeed            are  the Lord      most high above      all   the earth

Cloud and darkness  are  his raiment;      his throne, jus -tice  and  right.
The skies pro     -     claim his justice;      all peoples         see  his glory.
[                                                                ]      exalted far a - bove  all  spirits.

*omit in verse 3*

# Psalm 97 (98) – All the ends of the earth have seen salvation

## EXTRACT A – vv. 1-6

> The Nativity of the Lord: Mass during the Day – response 1 (v. 3)
> Common Psalm for Christmas
> Immaculate Conception of the BVM (December 8) – response 2 (v. 1)

*Response 1 (for Christmas):*

All the ends of the earth have seen the sal - va - -tion of our God.

*Response 2 (for Immaculate Conception):*

Sing a new song to the Lord for he has worked won - -ders.

*First line of verse 1 is optional when preceded by Response 2*

1. [Sing a new song to the Lord for he has worked wonders.]
2. The Lord has made known his sal - vation; has shown his justice to the nations.
3. All the ends of the earth have seen the salvation of our God.
4. Sing psalms to the Lord with the harp, with the sound of music.

His right hand and his ho - ly arm have brought sal - vation.
He has remembered his truth and love for the house of Israel.
Shout to the Lord, all the earth, ring out your joy.
With trumpets and the sound of the horn acclaim the King, the Lord.

# PSALM 97 (98)

## EXTRACT B – vv. 1-4. R/ cf v.2.

> 6th Sunday of Easter (Year B)
> 28th Sunday in Ordinary Time (Year C)

*Response:* The Lord__ has shown his sal - va - tion to the na - tions.

1. Sing a new song                    to   the   Lord      for he                    has worked wonders.
2. The Lord has made known   his    sal - vation;      has shown his justice to     the      nations.
3. All the ends of the               earth have  seen      the salvation                of   our      God.

His right hand and his      ho - ly   arm       have   brought sal - vation.
He has remembered his truth and  love       for the   house   of   Israel.
Shout to the Lord,            all   the  earth,       ring      out   your   joy.

## EXTRACT C – vv. 5-9. R/ cf v.9.

> 33rd Sunday in Ordinary Time (Year C)

*Response:* The   Lord comes to     rule the peo-ples with   fair-ness.

1. Sing psalms to the Lord with the harp, with the sound of music.
2. Let the sea and all with - in it thunder, the world and all its peoples.
3. For the Lord comes, he comes to rule the earth.

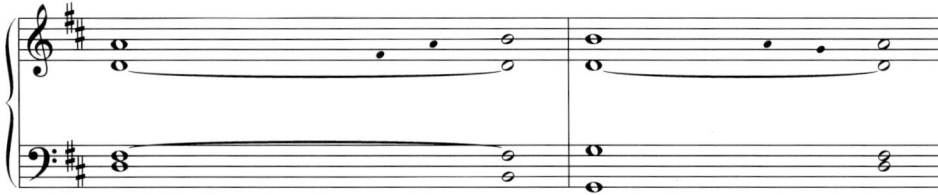

With trumpets and the sound of the horn acclaim the King, the Lord.
Let the rivers clap their hands and the hills ring out their joy at the presence of the Lord.
He will rule the world with justice and the peo - ples with fairness.

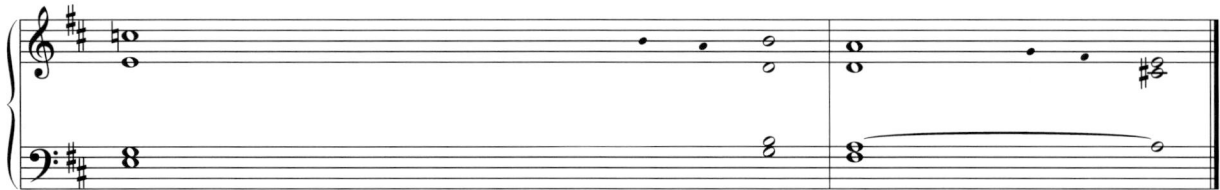

## Psalm 99 (100) – A song of joyful praise

R/ v. 3

> 11th Sunday of Ordinary Time (Year A)
> 4th Sunday of Easter (Year C)
> Common Psalm 6 for Ordinary Time

Response: **We are his peo - ple, the sheep— of his flock.**

1. Cry out with joy to the Lord, all the earth. Serve the Lord with gladness.
2. Know that he, the Lord is God. He made us, we be - long to him,
*3. Go within his gates, giv - ing thanks. Enter his courts with songs of praise.
4. Indeed, how good is the Lord, eternal his mer - ci - ful love.

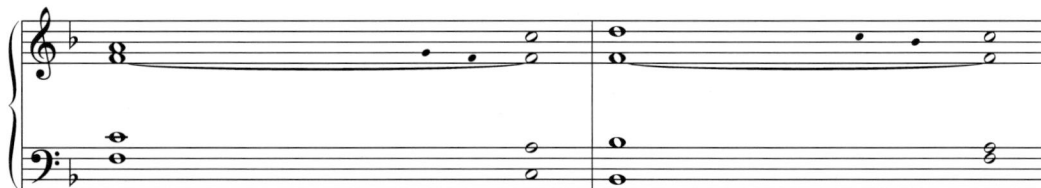

Come before him, sing - ing for joy.
we are his people, the sheep of his flock.
*Give thanks to him and bless— his name.
He is faithful from age— to age.

*– This verse is not given in the Lectionary,
but is included here to complete the psalm.

# Psalm 102 (103) – The Lord forgives all your sins

## EXTRACT A – vv. 1-4, 9-12. R/ v. 8

| 7th Sunday in Ordinary Time (Year A) – response 1 | 8th Sunday in Ordinary Time (Year B) – response 1 |
|---|---|
| 24th Sunday in Ordinary Time (Year A) – response 2 | 7th Sunday in Ordinary Time (Year C) – response 1 |

*Response 1 (all except 24th Sunday in O.T.):*         The    Lord is com-pas-sion and    love.__

*Response 2 (24th Sunday in O.T.):*

The    Lord is com-pas-sion and    love,__      slow to an-ger and rich__ in     mer-cy.__

1. My soul, give thanks        to    the Lord,     all my being, bless his    ho - ly    name.
2. It is he who forgives       all   your guilt,     who heals every one     of   your    ills,
3. His wrath will come        to    an   end;     he will not be ang   -   ry   for    ever.
4. For as the heavens are high a-bove the earth     so strong is his love for those who fear him.

My soul, give thanks        to    the Lord     and never forget      all    his blessings.
who redeems your life       from the grave,     who crowns you with love   and   com - passion.
He does not treat us according   to   our sins     nor repay us according      to    our    faults.
As far as the east is        from the west,     so far does he re     -    move our    sins.

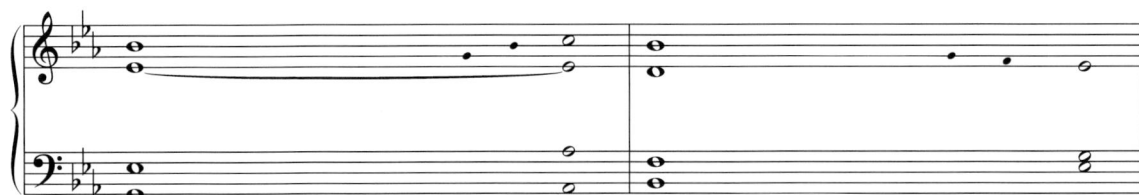

PSALM 102 (103)

EXTRACT B – vv. 1-4, 6-8, 11. R/ v. 8

3rd Sunday of Lent (Year C)

*Response:*  **The   Lord is com-pas-sion and    love.**__

1. My soul, give thanks    to    the Lord,    all my being, bless his       ho - ly   name.
2. It is he who forgives    all   your guilt,    who heals every one       of  your   ills,
3. The Lord does        deeds  of  justice,    gives judgement for all who are   op - pressed.
4. The Lord is compas - sion  and  love,    slow to an- ger and        rich  in   mercy.

My soul, give thanks        to  the  Lord    and never forget        all   his blessings.
who redeems your life        from the grave,    who crowns you with love  and  com - passion.
He made known his        ways  to Moses    and his deeds to Is       -    ra - el's   sons.
For as the heavens are high a-bove the  earth    so strong is his love for    those who fear him.

EXTRACT C – vv. 1-4, 8, 10, 12-13. R/ v. 8

Common Psalm 7 for Ordinary Time

*Response and verses 1, 2 & 4 from Extract B above, with the following final verse:*

4. As far as the east is from the west      so far does he re-move our sins.

As a father has compassion on his sons,      the Lord has pity on those who fear him.

87

# PSALM 102 (103)

## EXTRACT D – vv. 1-2, 11-12, 19-20. R/ v. 19

7th Sunday of Easter (Year B)

*Response:* **The Lord has set his sway— in hea-ven.**

*NOTE: The ICEL version of this response reads:*
*'The Lord has set his throne in heaven'.*

1. My soul, give thanks to the Lord,    all my being, bless his    ho - ly name.
2. For as the heavens are high a-bove the earth    so strong is his love for    those who fear him.
3. The Lord has set his    sway in heaven    and his kingdom is ruling ov - er all.

My soul, give thanks to the Lord    and never forget    all his blessings.
As far as the east is from the west,    so far does he re - move our sins.
Give thanks to the Lord, all his angels,    mighty in power, fulfill - ing his word.

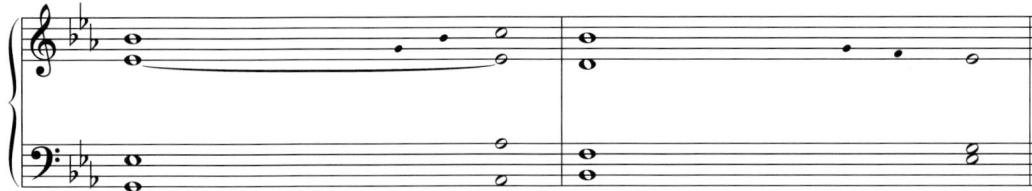

## EXTRACT E – vv. 1-4, 6-8, 10. R/ v. 17

Sacred Heart (Year A)

*Response:* **The love of the Lord is ev - er - las - -ting up-on those who hold him in fear.—**

1. My soul, give thanks to the Lord,    all my being, bless his    ho - ly name.
2. It is he who forgives all your guilt,    who heals every one    of your ills,
3. The Lord does deeds of justice,    gives judgement for all who are op - pressed.
4. The Lord is compas - sion and love,    slow to an- ger and rich in mercy.

My soul, give thanks to the Lord and never forget all his blessings.
who redeems your life from the grave, who crowns you with love and com-passion.
He made known his ways to Moses and his deeds to Is - ra-el's sons.
He does not treat us according to our sins nor repay us according to our faults.

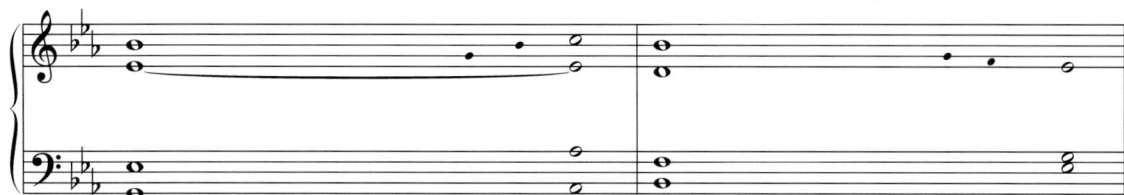

# Psalm 103 (104) – God's care for his creation

### EXTRACT A – vv. 1-2, 5-6, 10, 12-14, 24, 35. R/ cf v. 30

Easter Vigil (after the 1st reading)

*Response:* **Send forth your spi-rit, O Lord, and re-new the face of the earth.**

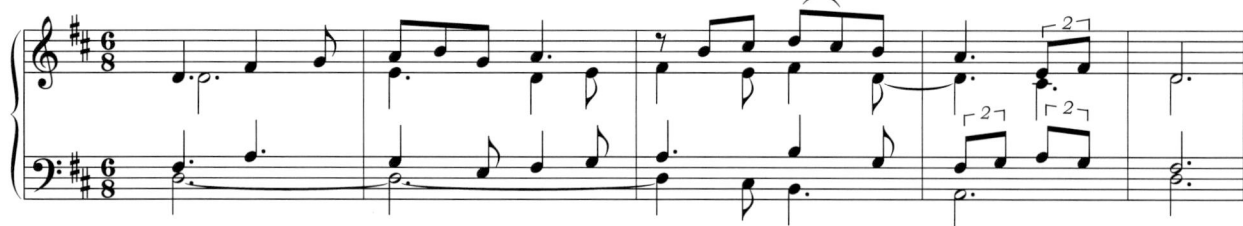

1. Bless the Lord, my soul! Lord God, how great you are,
2. You founded the earth on its base, to stand firm from age to age.
3. You make springs gush forth in the valleys: they flow in be - tween the hills.
4. From your dwelling you wa - ter the hills; earth drinks its fill of your gift.
5. How many are your works, O Lord! In wisdom you have made them all.

clothed in majes - ty and glory, wrapped in light as in a robe!
You wrapped it with the ocean like a cloak: the waters stood higher than the mountains.
On their banks dwell the birds of heaven; from the branches they sing their song.
You make the grass grow for the cattle and the plants to serve man's needs.
The earth is full of your riches. Bless the Lord, my soul.

# PSALM 103 (104)

## EXTRACT B – vv. 1-4, 24-25, 27-30. R/ v. 1

Baptism of the Lord (Year C)

*Response:* **Bless the Lord, my soul! Lord God, how great you are.**

### Verses 1, 4 & 5

1. Bless the      Lord, my soul!    clothed in majes - ty and glory,
4. All of these      look to you    to give them their food    in due season.
5. You take back your spi - rit, they die,    returning to the dust from which they came.

     wrapped in light as      in a robe!    You stretch our the heavens like a tent.
     You give it, they ga - ther it up:    you open your hand, they have their fill.
     You send forth your spirit, they are cre-ated,    and you renew the face of the earth.

### Verses 2 & 3

2. A- bove the rains you build your dwelling.    You make the clouds your chariot,
3. How many are your works, O Lord!    In wisdom you have made them all.

     you walk on the wings of the wind,    [      ]
     The earth is full of your riches.    There is the sea, vast and wide,

*omit in verse 2*

     you make the winds your messengers and flashing fire your servants.
     with its moving swarms past counting, liv- ing things great and small.

PSALM 103 (104)

EXTRACT C – vv. 1-2, 24, 27-30, 35. R/ cf v. 30

Pentecost Vigil (after 4th reading)
Pentecost Vigil (Simple Form)

*Response:* **Send forth your spi-rit, O Lord, and re-new__ the face of the earth.**

1. Bless the     Lord, my soul!    Lord God, how    great you are.
2. How many are your   works, O Lord!    In wisdom you have   made them all.
3. All of these     look to you    to give them their food   in due season.
4. You take back your spi - rit, they die,   returning to the dust from which they came.

clothed in majes     -     ty and glory    wrapped in light as    in a robe!
The earth is full     of your riches.    Bless the    Lord, my soul.
You give it, they ga   -   ther it up:   you open your hand, they have their fill.
You send forth your spirit, they are cre - ated,   and you renew the face   of the earth.

EXTRACT D – vv. 1, 24, 29-31, 34. R/ cf v. 30

Pentecost Sunday

*Response 'Send forth your spirit...' as above.*

1. Bless the     Lord, my soul!    Lord God, how    great you are.
2. You take back your spi - rit, they die,   returning to the dust from which they came.
3. May the glory of the Lord last for ever!   May the Lord rejoice   in his works!

clothed in majes     -     ty and glory    wrapped in light as    in a robe!
You send forth your spirit, they are cre-ated,   and you renew the face of   the earth.
May my thoughts be pleas - ing to him.   I find my joy    in the Lord.

91

## Psalm 104 (105) – Make know his deeds among the peoples

vv. 1-6, 8-9. R/ vv. 7-8

Holy Family (Year B option)

*Response:* **He, the Lord, is our God.** He re - mem - bers his co - ve - nant for ev - er.

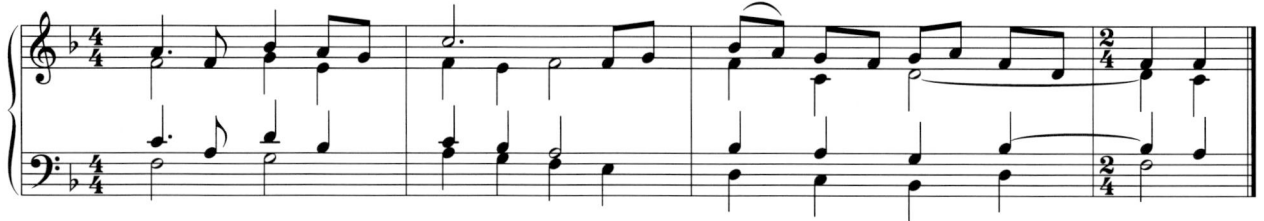

1. Give thanks to the Lord, tell his name, make known his deeds a-mong all the peoples.
2. Be proud of his ho - ly name, let the hearts that seek the Lord re - joice.
3. Remember the wonders he has done, his miracles, the judge - ments he spoke.
4. He remembers his cove -nant for ever, his promise to a thousand ge - ne-rations,

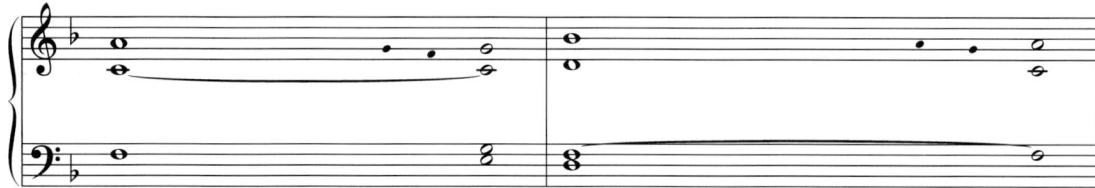

O sing to him, sing his praise; tell all his won - der - ful works.
Consider the Lord and his strength; constantly seek his face.
O children of Abra -ham his servant, O sons of the Ja - cob he chose.
the covenant he made with Abraham, the oath he swore to Isaac.

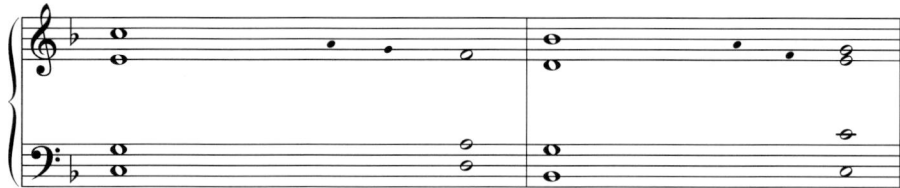

*Blessed be the Lord, God of Israel,*

*for ever, from age to age.*

*Let all the people cry out:*

*'Amen! Amen! Alleluia!'*

*Psalm 105:48*
*The Conclusion of Book 4*

# BOOK 5

PSALMS 106 (107) – 150

# Psalm 106 (107) – Rescued by the Lord

EXTRACT A – vv. 2-9. R/ v. 1

Pentecost Vigil (after the 3rd reading)

*Response:* **O give thanks to the Lord, for he___ is good; for his love___ has no end.**

1. Let them say this, the Lord's re - deemed,
2. Some wandered in the desert, in the wilderness,
3. Then they cried to the Lord in their need
4. Let them thank the Lord for his love,

whom he redeemed from the hand of the foe
finding no way to a city they could dwell in.
and he rescued them from their dis - tress
for the wonders he does for men.

and gathered from far - off lands, from east and west, from north and south.
Hungry they were and thirsty; their soul was faint - ing with - in them.
and he led them a - long the right way, to reach a city they could dwell in.
For he satisfies the thir - sty soul; he fills the hun - gry with good things.

EXTRACT B – vv. 23-26, 28-31. R/ v. 1

12th Sunday in Ordinary Time (Year B)

*Response:* **O give thanks to the Lord, for his love en - dures for ev - er.**

94

1. Some sailed to the sea in ships to trade on the migh-ty waters.
2. For he spoke; he sum - moned the gale, tossing the waves of the sea
3. Then they cried to the Lord in their need and he rescued them from their dis - tress
4. They rejoiced because of the calm and he led them to the haven they de - sired.

These men have seen the Lord's deeds, the wonders he does in the deep.
up to heaven and back in -to the deep; their soul melted away in their dis - tress.
He stilled the storm to a whisper: all the waves of the sea were hushed.
Let them thank the Lord for his love, the wonders he does for men.

## Psalm 109 (110) – The Lord's priestly revelation

vv. 1-4. R/ v. 4

Corpus Christi (Year C)

*Response:* **You are a priest for ev - - er,___ a priest like Mel-chi-ze-dek of old.**

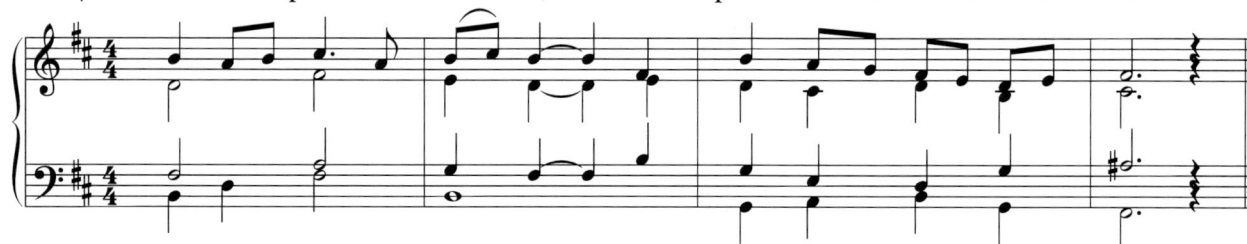

1. The Lord's revelation to my Master: 'Sit on my right:
2. The Lord will send from Zion your scep - tre of power:
3. A prince on the day of your birth on the ho - ly mountains;
4. The Lord has sworn an oath he will not change. 'You are a priest for ever,

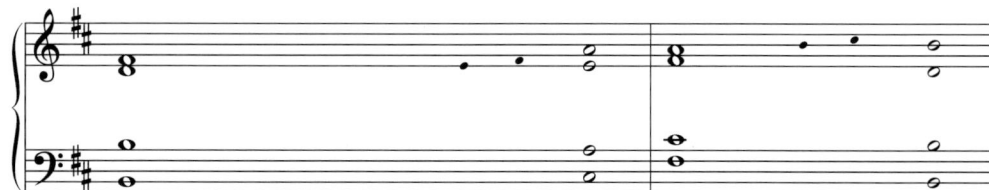

I will put your foes be - neath your feet.'
rule in the midst of all your foes.
from the womb before the dawn I be - got you.
a priest like Melchize - dek of old.'

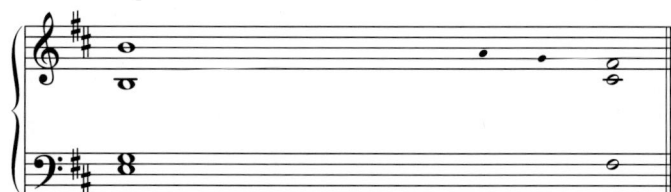

# Psalm 111 (112) – Blessed the one who fears the Lord

vv. 4-9. R/ v. 3

5th Sunday in Ordinary Time (Year A)

*Response:* The good man is a light in the dark-ness for the up--right.

1. He is a light in the darkness for the upright: he is generous, merci - ful and just.
2. The just man will nev-er waver: he will be remem - bered for ever.
3. With a steadfast heart he will not fear; open-handed, he gives to the poor;

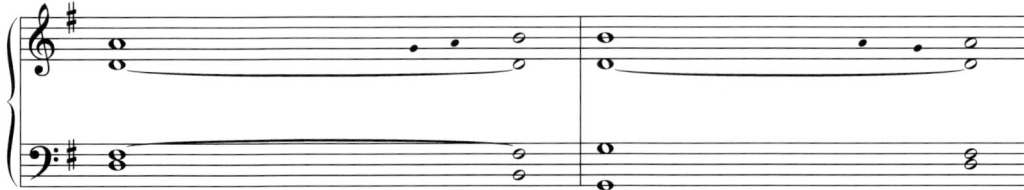

The good man takes pi - ty and lends, he conducts his af - fairs with honour.
He has no fear of e - vil news; with a firm heart he trusts in the Lord.
his justice stands firm for ever. His head will be raised in glory.

# Psalm 112 (113) – The Lord lifts up the lowly

vv. 1-2, 4-8. R/ cf vv. 1, 7

25th Sunday in Ordinary Time (Year C)

*Response:* **Praise the Lord, who rai - ses the poor.**

1. Praise, O servants of the Lord, praise the name of the Lord!
2. High above all nations is the Lord, above the hea - vens his glory.
3. From the dust he lifts up the lowly, from the dung-heap he rai -ses the poor

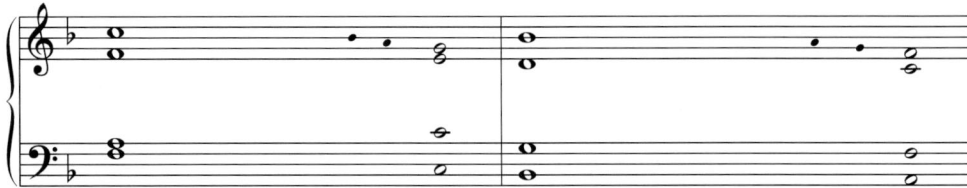

[                                              ]
Who is like the Lord, our God, who has risen on high to his throne
[                                              ]

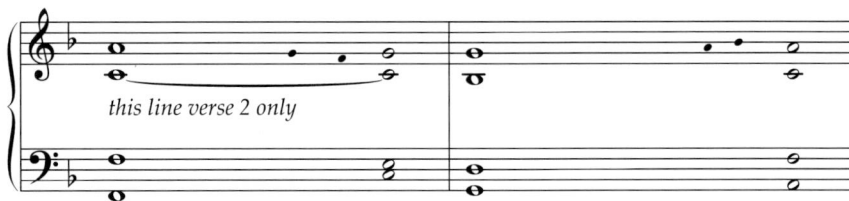

*this line verse 2 only*

May the name of the Lord be blessed both now and for ev - er - more!
yet stoops from the heights to look down, to look down upon hea-ven and earth?
to set him in the compa - ny of princes, yes, with the princes of his people.

97

# Psalm 114-115 (116) – I love the Lord, for he has heard my cry

EXTRACT A – (Ps 114) vv. 1-6, 8-9. R/ v. 9

24th Sunday in Ordinary Time (Year B)

*Response:* I will walk in the pre - sence of the Lord in the land__ of the liv - - ing.__

1. I love the Lord for he has heard the cry of my ap - peal;
2. They surrounded me, the snares of death, with the anguish of the tomb;
3. How gracious is the Lord, and just; our God has com - passion.
4. He has kept my soul from death, my eyes from tears and my feet from stumbling.

*This line for verse 2 only*
they caught me, sorrow and dis-tress.

for he turned his ear to me in the day when I called him.
I called on the Lord's name. O Lord my God, de - liver me!
The Lord protects the sim - ple hearts; I was helpless so he saved me.
I will walk in the presence of the Lord in the land of the living.

EXTRACT B – (Ps 115) vv. 10, 15-19. R/ (Ps 114) v. 9

2nd Sunday of Lent (Year B)

*Response: 'I will walk...' as above*

1. I trusted, even when I said: 'I am sore - ly af-flicted.'
2. Your servant, Lord, your ser-vant am I; you have loo-sened my bonds.
3. My vows to the Lord I will ful - fil before all his people,

98

PSALM 114-115 (116)

O precious in the eyes　　　of the Lord　　is the death of　　his　faithful.
A thanksgiving sacri　-　fice I　make;　　I will call on the Lord's　name.
in the courts of the house　of the Lord,　　in your midst, O　Je - rusalem.

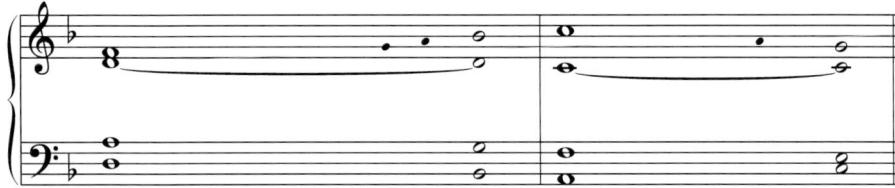

EXTRACT C – (Ps 115) vv. 12-13, 15-18

Maundy Thursday (Evening Mass) – response 1 (1 Cor 10:16)
Corpus Christi (Year B) – response 2 (v. 13)

*Response 1 (Maundy Thursday):*

The　bless-ing cup that we　bless　　is　a comm - un-ion with the blood of　　Christ.

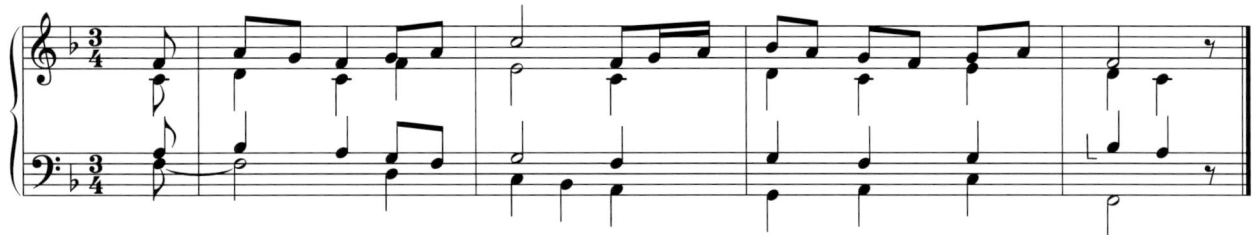

*Response 2 (Corpus Christi):*

The　cup of sal-va-tion I will　raise;　　I will　call＿ on the Lord's＿　name.

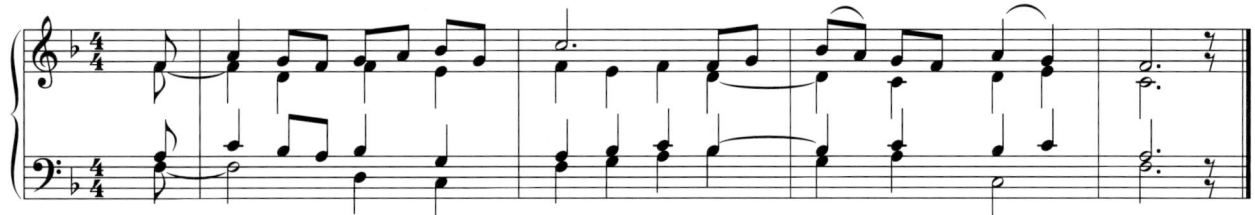

1.　How can I re　-　pay the Lord　　for his good -ness　to　me?
2.　O precious in the eyes　of the Lord　　is the death　of　his　faithful.
3.　A thanksgiving sacri - fice I　make;　　I will call on　the Lord's　name.

The cup of salvation　　　I　will raise;　　I will call on the　　Lord's　name.
Your servant, Lord, your ser-vant am　I;　　you have loosened　my　bonds.
My vows to the Lord I　　　will ful - fil　　before all　　　　his　people.

99

# Psalm 116 (117) – O praise the Lord, all you nations

R/ Mk 16:15

> 9th Sunday in Ordinary Time (Year C) – response 1
> 21st Sunday in Ordinary Time (Year C) – response 1
> St Patrick (March 17 – in Ireland) – response 2

*Response 1 (for 9th and 21st Sundays):*

Go out to the whole world___ and pro - claim the Good News.___

*Response 2 (for St Patrick):*

Go out to all___ the world___ and tell the Good News.___

V. O praise the Lord, all you na-tions,___ ac - claim___ him all you peo-ples!

Strong is his love for us; he is faith - ful for ev - er.___

# Psalm 117 (118) – Processional Song of Praise

### EXTRACT A – vv. 1-2, 16-17, 22-23

Easter Vigil (psalm after the Epistle reading) – response 1
Easter Sunday & Common Psalm 1 for Eastertide – response 2 (v. 24)

*EASTER VIGIL: The priest or psalmist intones three times in ascending keys and all repeat each time:*

Al - le - - - - - -lu - - - ia._____

Al - le - - - - - - -lu - - - ia._____

Al - le - - - - - - lu - - - ia._____

*or alternatively:*

Al - le - lu - ia,      al - le - lu - ia,____      al - le - lu - ia.

*Psalmist/Cantor:*

1.  Give thanks to the Lord for  he   is      good,      for his love      has   no      end.
2.  The Lord's right              hand has triumphed;   his                 right hand raised me.
3.  The stone which the buil - ders re - jected      has become the  cor - ner - stone.

Let the sons of Isra - el   say:       'His love   has   no   end.'
I shall not die, I      shall live       and re - count his deeds.
This is the work of the Lord,       a marvel   in   our eyes.

PSALM 117 (118)

*EASTER SUNDAY*

*Response:* **This___ day was made by the Lord; we___ re-joice and are glad.**

1. Give thanks to the Lord for he is good, for his love has no end.
2. The Lord's right hand has triumphed; his right hand raised me.
3. The stone which the buil - ders re - jected has become the cor - ner - stone.

Let the sons of Isra - el say: 'His love has no end.'
I shall not die, I shall live and re - count his deeds.
This is the work of the Lord, a marvel in our eyes.

EXTRACT B – vv. 2-4, 13-18, 22-27. R/ v. 1

2nd Sunday of Easter

*Response:* **Give thanks to the Lord for he__ is good, for his love__ has__ no end.**

*This response is used every year, but with different extracts from Psalm 117 for each year of the Lectionary cycle*

**Year A**

1. Let the sons of Is - ra - el say: 'His love has no end.'
2. I was thrust, thrust down and falling but the Lord was my helper.
3. The stone which the buil - ders re - jected has become the cor-ner-stone.

Let the sons of Aa - ron say: 'His love has no end.'
The Lord is my strength and my song; he was my saviour.
This is the work of the Lord, a marvel in our eyes.

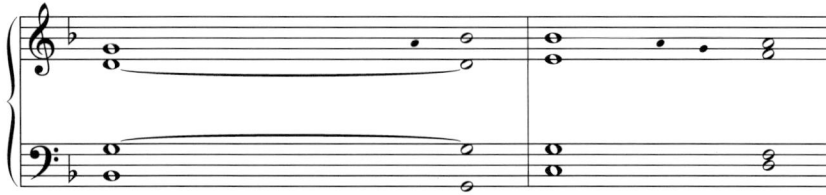

Let those who fear the Lord say: 'His love has no end.'
There are shouts of joy and victory in the tents of the just.
This day was made by the Lord; we rejoice and are glad.

*Year B*

1. Let the sons of Is - ra - el say: 'His love has no end.'
2. The Lord's right hand has triumphed; his right hand raised me.
3. The stone which the buil-ders re - jected has become the cor - ner - stone.

Let the sons of Aa - ron say: 'His love has no end.'
I shall not die, I shall live and re - count his deeds.
This is the work of the Lord, a marvel in our eyes.

Let those who fear the Lord say: 'His love has no end.'
I was punished, I was punished by the Lord, but not doomed to die.
This day was made by the Lord; we rejoice and are glad.

*Year C overleaf*

PSALM 117 (118)

EXTRACT B – vv. 2-4, 13-18, 22-27. R/ v. 1 (continued)

2nd Sunday of Easter (Year C)

*Response:* Give thanks to the Lord for he __ is good, for his love __ has __ no end.

**Year C**

1. Let the sons of Is - ra - el say: 'His love has no end.'
2. The stone which the buil-ders re-jected has become the cor - ner-stone.
3. O Lord, grant us sal-vation; O Lord, grant suc-cess.

Let the sons of Aa - ron say: 'His love has no end.'
This is the work of the Lord, a marvel in our eyes.
Blessed in the name of the Lord is he who comes.

Let those who fear the Lord say: 'His love has no end.'
This day was made by the Lord; we rejoice and are glad.
We bless you from the house of the Lord; the Lord God is our light.

104

## EXCERPT C – vv. 1, 8-9, 21-23, 26, 28-29. R/ v. 22

4th Sunday of Easter (Year B)

*Response:* The stone which the buil-ders re - jec-ted___ has be - come the cor-ner - - stone.

1. Give thanks to the Lord for he is good, for his love has no end.
2. I will thank you for you have gi-ven answer and you are my saviour.
3. Blessed in the name of the Lord is he who comes. We bless you in the house of the Lord.

It is better to take refuge in the Lord than to trust in men:
The stone which the builders re - jected has become the cor-ner - stone.
*You are my God, I thank you. My God, I praise you.

*- The text in this line is a correction to the text given in the Lectionary*

it is better to take refuge in the Lord than to trust in princes.
This is the work of the Lord, a marvel in our eyes.
Give thanks to the Lord for he is good, for his love has no end.

# Psalm 118 (119) – Blessed are those whose ways are blameless

EXCERPT A – vv. 1-2, 4-5, 17-18, 33-34. R/ v. 1

6th Sunday in Ordinary Time (Year A)

*Response:* **They are hap-py who fol-low God's law!**

1. They are happy whose life is blameless, who fol - low God's law!
2. You have laid down your precepts to be o - beyed with care.
3. Bless your servant and I shall live and o - bey your word.
4. Teach me the demands of your statutes and I will keep them to the end.

They are happy those who do his will, seek-ing him with all their hearts.
May my foot - steps be firm to o - bey your statutes.
Open my eyes that I may con-sider the wonders of your law.
Train me to ob - serve your law, to keep it with my heart.

EXCERPT B – vv. 57, 72, 76-77, 127-130. R/ v. 97

17th Sunday in Ordinary Time (Year A)

*Response:* **Lord, how I love your___ law!**

1. My part, I have re - solved, O Lord, is to o - bey your word.
2. Let your love be ready to con-sole me by your promise to your servant.
3. That is why I love your com-mands more than fi - nest gold.
4. Your will is wonder - ful in - deed; therefore I o - bey it.

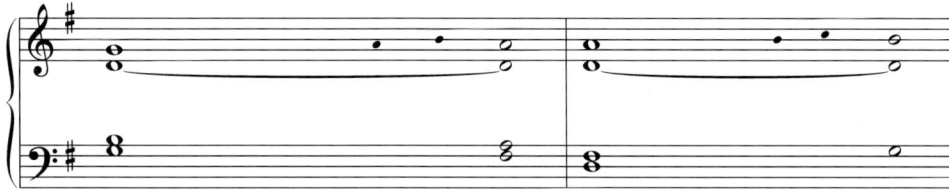

The law from your mouth means more to me than sil - ver and gold.
Let your love come to me and I shall live for your law is my de - light.
That is why I rule my life by your precepts: I hate false ways.
The unfolding of your word gives light and tea - ches the simple.

## Psalm 120 (121) – I lift up my eyes to the mountains

R/ cf v. 2

29th Sunday in Ordinary Time (Year C)

Response: **Our help is in the name of the Lord who made hea-ven and earth.**

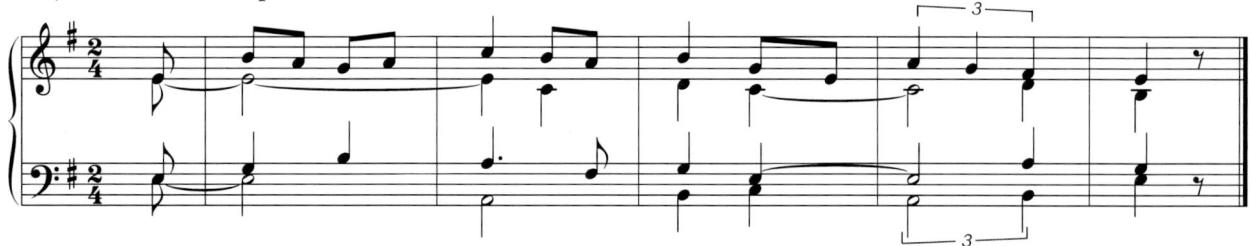

1. I lift up my eyes to the mountains: from where shall come my help?
2. May he never allow you to stumble! Let him sleep not, your guard.
3. The Lord is your guard and your shade; at your right side he stands.
4. The Lord will guard you from evil, he will guard your soul.

My help shall come from the Lord who made hea-ven and earth.
No, he sleeps not nor slumbers, Is - ra - el's guard.
By day the sun shall not smite you nor the moon in the night.
The Lord will guard your go -ing and coming both now and for ever.

107

# Psalm 121 (122) – Pray for the peace of Jerusalem

EXTRACT A – vv. 1-2, 4-5, 6-9. R/ cf v. 1

1st Sunday of Advent (Year A)
Common Psalm 9 for Ordinary Time (last weeks)

*Response:* I re - joiced when I heard them say: 'Let us go to God's___ house.'

*The psalmist continues:*

1. ...and now our feet are standing   with- in your gates, O Je-rusalem.

2. It is there that the   tribes go   up,   the tribes   of   the   Lord.
3. For the peace of Jeru - sa - lem pray:   'Peace be   to   your homes!
4. For love of my breth - ren   and friends   I say:   'Peace up- on you!'

For Israel's law it is   there to praise the Lord's name.
[   ]
[   ]

*this line is for verse 2 only*

There were set the   thrones of judgement   of the   house of David.
May peace reign   in   your   walls,   in your pa - la - ces, peace!'
For love of the house   of   the   Lord   I will ask   for   your good.

108

# PSALM 121 (122)

## EXTRACT B – vv. 1-5. R/ cf v. 1

Christ the King (Year C)

*Response:* I re - joiced when I heard them say: 'Let us go to God's__ house.'

*The psalmist continues:*

1. ...and now our feet are standing   with- in your gates, O Je-rusalem.

2. Jerusalem is built as a city   strong - ly com - pact.
3. For Israel's   law it is   there to praise the Lord's name

It is there that the tribes go   up   the tribes   of   the Lord.
There were set the thrones of judgement of the   house of Israel.

# Psalm 122 (123) – To you have I lifted up my eyes

R/ v. 2

14th Sunday in Ordinary Time (Year B)

*Response:* **Our** eyes are on the **Lord till he** show us his mer - cy.

1. To you have I lifted up my eyes, you who dwell in the heavens:
2. Like the eyes of a servant on the hand of her mistress,
3. Have mercy on us, Lord, have mercy. We are filled with con - tempt.

my eyes, like the eyes of slaves on the hand of their lords.
so our eyes are on the Lord our God till he show us his mercy.
Indeed all too full is our soul with the scorn of the rich, with the proud man's dis - dain.

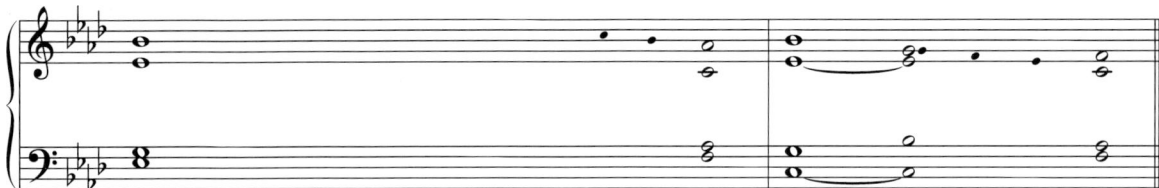

110

# Psalm 125 (126) – We thought we were dreaming

> 30th Sunday of Ordinary Time (Year B) – response 1 (v. 3)
> 2nd Sunday of Advent (Year C) – response 1
> 5th Sunday of Lent (Year C) – response 1
> St George (April 23 – in England) – response 2 (v. 5)

*Response 1 (for given Sundays):*  What mar- vels the Lord worked for us! In - deed we were glad.

*Response 2 (for St George):*  Those who are sow-ing in tears will sing when they reap.

1. When the Lord delivered Zion from bondage    it seemed like a    dream.
2. The heathens themselves said: 'What marvels    the Lord worked for    them!'
3. Deliver us, O Lord, from our    bondage    as streams in dry    land.
4. They go out, they go out, full of    tears    carrying seed for the sowing:

Then was our mouth filled with    laughter,    on our lips there were songs.
What marvels the Lord worked for    us!    In- deed we    were glad.
Those who are sowing in    tears    will sing when    they    reap.
they come back, they come back, full of song,    carrying    their sheaves.

# Psalm 127 (128) – Your wife like a fruitful vine

Holy Family (Year A) – response 1
33rd Sunday in Ordinary Time (Year A) – response 2
27th Sunday in Ordinary Time (Year B) – response 3

*Response 1 (Holy Family):*

O bless - èd are those who fear the Lord and walk in his ways!

*Response 2 (33rd Sunday in Ordinary Time (A)):*

O bless - èd are those who fear____ the Lord.

*Response 3 (27th Sunday in Ordinary Time (B)):*

May the Lord bless____ us all the days____ of our lives.

*The first line of the first verse may be omitted on the feast of the Holy Family, as it duplicates the refrain.*

1. O blessèd are those who fear the Lord     and walk in     his ways!
2. Your wife like a     fruit-ful vine     in the heart of     your house;
3. Indeed thus     shall be blest     the man who fears the Lord.

By the labour of your hands you shall eat.     You will be happy and prosper.
your children like shoots of     the olive     around     your table.
May the Lord bless you     from Zion     all the days of     your life.*

*\* – On Sundays of Ordinary Time, verse 3 is continued on the next page.*

112

*Continuation of verse 3 on Sundays in Ordinary Time:*

May you see your child-ren's children      in a happy Je-rusalem.

## Psalm 129 (130) – Out of the depths

R/ v. 7

| 5th Sunday of Lent (Year A) |
| 10th Sunday of Ordinary Time (Year B) |
| Common Psalm 3 for Lent |

*Response:* **With the      Lord there is      mer - - cy      and      full-ness of re - demp - -tion._____**

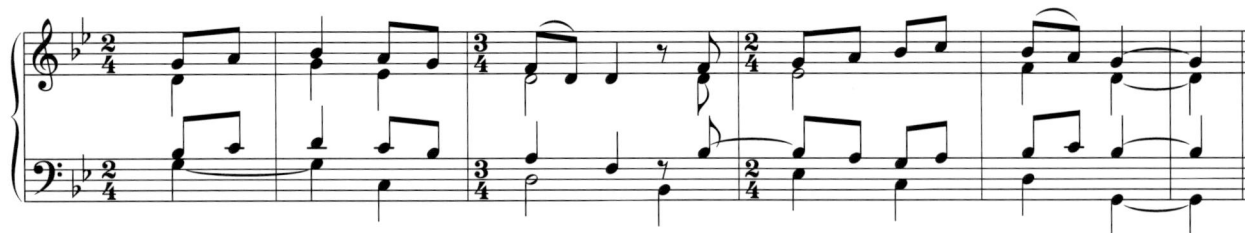

1.  Out of the depths I cry to you, O  Lord,      Lord, hear my            voice!
2.  If you, O Lord, should mark our  guilt,      Lord, who would sur - vive?
3.  My soul is waiting for the            Lord,      I count on his            word.
4.  Because with the Lord there is  mercy      and fullness of re - demption.

O let your ears be at    -    tentive      to the voice of            my  pleading.
But with you is found for-giveness:      for this we            re - vere you.
My soul is longing for the     Lord      more than watchman for daybreak.*
Israel indeed he will re   -   deem      from all its            in - iquity.

*\* – Verse 3 continued on next line
(except on 10th Sunday in O.T.)*

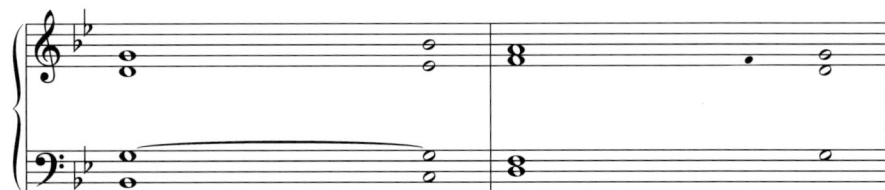

(Let the watch- man count on daybreak    and Israel on the Lord.)

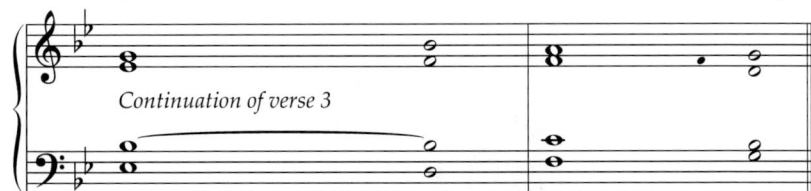

*Continuation of verse 3*

# Psalm 130 (131) – God as mother

31st Sunday in Ordinary Time (Year A)

*Response:* **Keep my soul in peace be - fore you, O Lord.**

1. O Lord, my heart is not proud, nor haugh - ty my eyes.
2. Tru- ly I have set my soul in si - lence and peace.

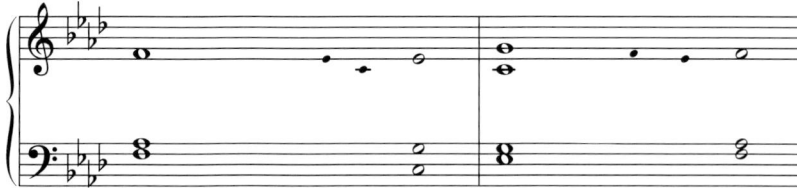

I have not gone af- ter things too great nor mar - vels be-yond me.
A weaned child on its mo - ther's breast, even so is my soul.

3. O Is- ra- el, hope in the Lord both now and for ever.

# Psalm 131 (132) – O Lord, remember David

vv. 6-7, 9-10, 13-14. R/ v. 8

The Assumption of the BVM (Vigil – August 14)

*Response:* **Go up, Lord, to the place of your rest, you and the ark of your strength.**

1. At Ephrata we heard of the ark; we found it in the plains of Yearim.
2. Your priests shall be clothed with holiness: your faithful shall ring out their joy.
3. For the Lord has cho - sen Zion; he has desired it for his dwelling:

'Let us go to the place of his dwelling; let us go to kneel at his footstool.'
For the sake of Da - vid your servant do not reject your an - ointed.
'This is my resting place for ever, here have I cho - sen to live.'

# Psalm 135 (136) – For his love endures for ever

vv. 1-6 & 16-17, 21 or 24-26. R/ cf v. 1

Common Psalm for the Easter Vigil

*This psalm has an inbuilt refrain, which may be sung by a vocal group.*
*Alternatively, the whole assembly may sing this refrain, in which case the response may be omitted.*
*The Lectionary divides this psalm in two: verses 1-3 & 5 and verses 1-2 & 4.*

*Response:* **Great__ is his love, love with-out__ end.**

1. O give thanks to the Lord for he is good,
2. Who alone has wrought mar - vel - lous works,
3. It was he who made the great lights,
-----
4. Through the desert his peo - ple he led,
5. And he snatched us away from our foes,

**for his love__ en - dures__ for ev - - er.**
"
"
"
"

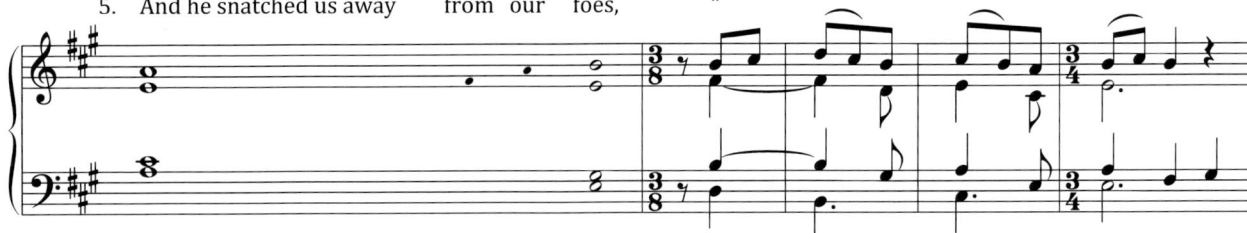

Give thanks to the God of gods,
whose wisdom it was made the skies,
the sun to rule in the day,
-----
Nations in their great - ness he struck,
He gives food to all liv - ing things,

**for his love__ en - dures__ for ev - - er.**
"
"
"
"

Give thanks to the Lord of lords,
who fixed the earth firmly on the seas,
the moon and stars in the night,
-----
He let Israel inher - it their hand,
To the God of hea - ven give thanks,

**for his love__ en - dures__ for ev - - er.**
"
"
"
"

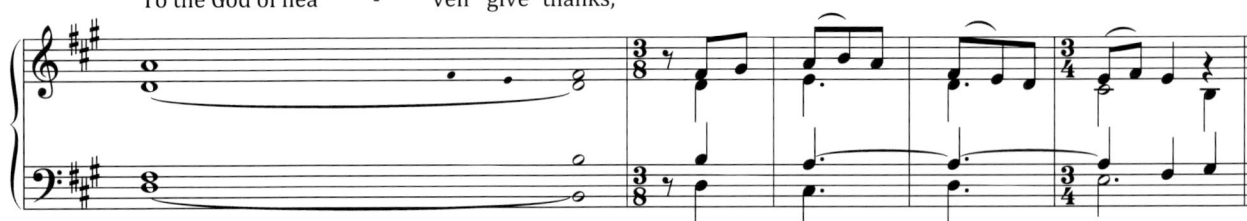

116

# Psalm 136 (137) – By the rivers of Babylon

## vv. 1-6

4th Sunday of Lent (Year B)

*Response:* O let my tongue cleave to my mouth if I re - mem - ber you not!

1. By the waters of Babylon there we       sat and wept,    remem - ber-ing Zion;
2. For it was there that they asked us, our cap-tors, for songs,    our oppres-sors, for joy.
3. O how could we sing the song        of the Lord    on a - li - en soil?
4. O let my tongue cleave          to my mouth    if I remem - ber you not!

on the pop-lars that grew there  we hung up our harps.
'Sing to   us,' they   said,    'one of   Zi - on's songs.'
If I forget  you, Je - rusalem,  let my  right hand wither!
if I prize  not Je - rusalem  above  all  my  joys!

# Psalm 137 (138) – I thank you, Lord, with all my heart

## EXTRACT A – vv. 1-3, 6, (7,) 8

21st Sunday in Ordinary Time (Year A) – response 1 (v. 8)
17th Sunday in Ordinary Time (Year C) – response 2 (cf v. 3)

Response 1
(21st Sunday): Your love, O Lord, is e - ter- -nal,_ dis - card_ not the work_ of your hands._

Response 2
(17th Sunday): On the day I called, you ans - wered me, O Lord.

* – On 21st Sunday in O.T., omit these lines: verse 3 ends with 'Your love...' and there is no verse 4.

1. I thank you, Lord, with        all   my   heart,     you have heard the words   of      my   mouth.
2. I thank you for your faithful - ness and   love      which excel all we ever     knew   of    you.
3. The Lord is high yet he looks on   the   lowly      and the haughty he knows from    a  -  far.
*4. You stretch out your right    hand and save me.    Your hand will do               all  things for me.

In the presence of the angels      I    will bless you.    I will adore before your        ho - ly  temple.
On the day I                       called, you answered;   you increased the strength  of   my   soul.
*Though I walk in the midst    of   af - fliction      you give me life and frus - trate my   foes.
Your love, O Lord,                 is    e - ternal,      discard not the work               of  your hands.

## EXTRACT B – vv. 1-5, 7-8. R/ v. 1

5th Sunday in Ordinary Time (Year C)

Response: Be - fore the   an - gels   I   will   bless   you,   O   Lord.

1. I thank you, Lord, with all my heart, you have heard the words of my mouth.
2. I thank you for your faithful-ness and love which excel all we ever knew of you.
3. All earth's kings shall thank you when they hear the words of your mouth.
4. You stretch out your right hand and save me. Your hand will do all things for me.

In the presence of the angels I will bless you. I will adore before your ho - ly temple.
On the day I called, you answered; you increased the strength of my soul.
They shall sing of the Lord's ways: 'How great is the glory of the Lord!'
Your love, O Lord, is e - ternal, discard not the work of your hands.

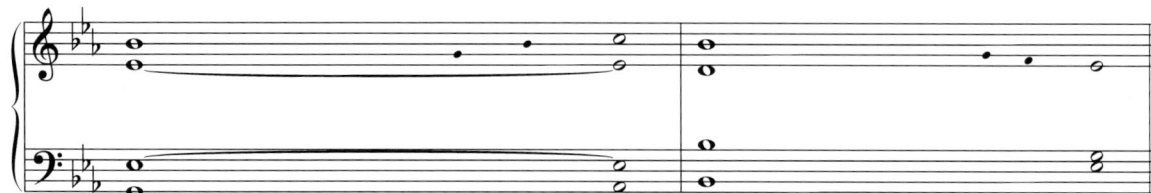

## Psalm 138 (139) – O Lord, you search me and you know me

vv. 1-3, 13-15. R/ v. 14

Nativity of St John the Baptist (Day – June 24)

*Response:* I thank you for the won-der of my be - ing.

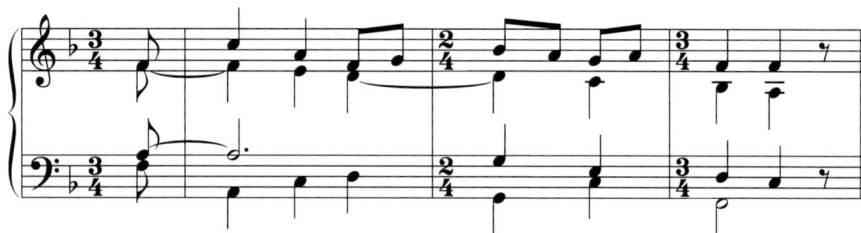

1. O Lord, you search me and you know me, you know my resting and my rising,
2. For it was you who crea -ted my being, knit me together in my mo-ther's womb.
3. Already you knew my soul, my body held no se - cret from you

you discern my purpose from a - far. You mark when I walk or lie down,
I thank you for the wonder of my being, [                    ]
when I was being fa - shioned in secret [                    ]

*verse 1 only*

all my ways lie o - pen to you.
for the wonders of all your cre-ation.
and moulded in the depths of the earth.

119

# Psalm 144 (145) – I shall praise you to the heights, God my King

EXTRACT A – vv. 1-2, 8-9, 10-11, 13-14. R/ v. 1

> 14th Sunday of Ordinary Time (Year A)
> 31st Sunday of Ordinary Time (Year C)
> Common Psalm 8 for Ordinary Time

*Response:* **I will bless your name for ev-er, O God my King.**

1. I will give you glory, O God my King, I will bless your name for ever.
2. The Lord is kind and full of com-passion, slow to anger, abound-ing in love.
3. The Lord is just in all his ways and loving in all his deeds.
4. The Lord is faithful in all his words and loving in all his deeds.

I will bless you day af - ter day, and praise your name for ever..
How good is the Lord to all, compassionate to all his creatures.
He is close to all who call him, and declare your from their hearts.
The Lord supports all who fall and raises all who are bowed down.

EXTRACT B – vv. 8-9 or 10-11, 15-18. R/ v. 16

> 18th Sunday in Ordinary Time (Year A)
> 17th Sunday in Ordinary Time (Year B)

*Response:* **You o-pen wide your hand, O Lord, you grant our de - sires.**

120

# PSALM 144 (145)

\* – On 18th Sunday in O.T. (Year A)

† – On 17th Sunday in O.T. (Year B)

\*1. The Lord is kind and full    of com-passion,    slow to anger, abound   -   ing   in   love.

†1. All your creatures shall thank you,   O   Lord,    and your friends shall re   -   peat their blessing.

-----

2. The eyes of all creatures    look   to   you    and you give them their food   in   due   time.

3. The Lord is just in    all   his   ways    and loving in    all   his   deeds.

\* How good is the    Lord   to   all,    compassionate to   all   his   creatures.

† They shall speak of the glory   of   your   reign    and declare your   might,   O   God,

-----

You open    wide your   hand    grant the desires of   all   who   live.

He is close to    all   who call him,    who call on him    from their   hearts.

## EXTRACT C – vv. 2-3, 8-9, 17-18. R/ v. 18

25th Sunday in Ordinary Time (Year A)

*Response:* **The Lord is    close to    all__ who__    call him.**

1. I will give you glory, O   God my   King,    I will bless your    name for ever.

2. The Lord is kind and full   of com-passion,    slow to anger, abound - ing   in   love.

3. The Lord is just in    all   his   ways    and loving in    all   his deeds.

The Lord is great, highly   to   be   praised,    his greatness can - not   be   measured.

How good is the    Lord   to   all,    compassionate to all   his   creatures.

He is close to    all   who call him,    who call on him   from their   hearts.

## EXTRACT D – vv. 8-13. R/ v. 1

5th Sunday of Easter (Year C)

*Response:* **I will bless— your name— for ev-er,   O   God— my King.——**

1. The Lord is kind and full          of com-passion,     slow to anger, abound - ing   in     love.
2. All your creatures shall thank you,  O    Lord,        and your friends shall re-peat their blessing.

How good is the            Lord  to   all,       compassionate to   all   his creatures.
They shall speak of the glory  of  your reign      and declare your  might, O     God,   *> continue on next line*

*Continuation of verse 2*

to make known to all your migh-ty deeds        and the glorious splendour of your name.

3. Yours is an ever-last-ing kingdom;    your rule lasts from age to age.

# Psalm 145 (146) – Praise the ever-faithful God

## EXTRACT A – vv. 6-10

3rd Sunday of Advent (Year A) – response 1 (cf Is 35:4)
4th Sunday of Ordinary Time (Year A) – response 2 (Mt 5:3)

*Response 1 (Advent):* **Come, Lord, and save us.**

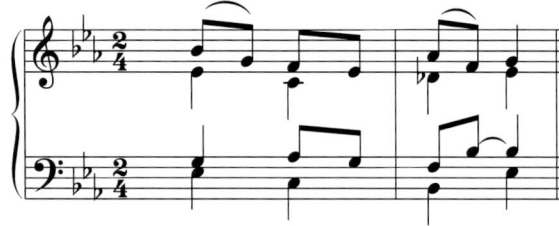

*Response 2 (Ordinary Time):*

How hap-py are the poor in spi - rit; theirs is the king- dom of hea-ven.

1. It is the Lord who keeps faith for ever, who is just to those who are op - pressed.
2. It is the Lord who gives sight to the blind, who raises up those who are bowed down,
3. It is the Lord who loves the just but thwarts the path of the wicked.

It is he who gives bread to the hungry, the Lord, who sets pri-son-ers free.
the Lord, who pro - tects the stranger, and upholds the wi - dow and orphan.
The Lord will reign for ever, Zion's God, from age to age.

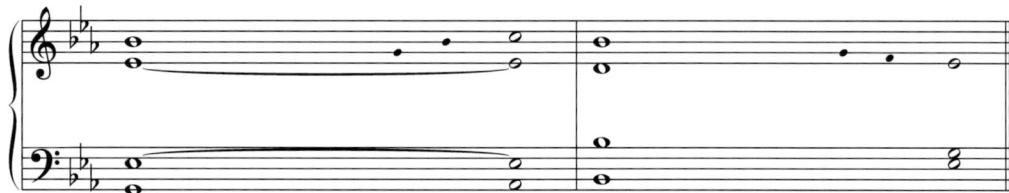

EXTRACT B – vv. 6-10 (alternative). R/ v. 8

23rd Sunday of Ordinary Time (Year B)
32nd Sunday of Ordinary Time (Year B)
26th Sunday of Ordinary Time (Year C)

*Response:* **My soul, give praise to the Lord.**

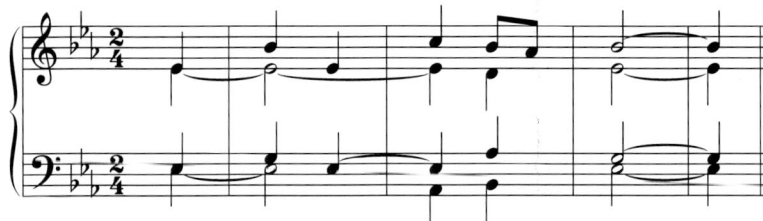

1. It is the Lord who keeps        faith for   ever,        who is just to those who  are   op - pressed.
2. It is the Lord who gives sight   to   the   blind,        who raises up those who are bowed  down,
3. The Lord upholds the wi   -   dow and orphan        but thwarts the path        of   the   wicked.

It is he who gives bread   to   the hungry,        the Lord, who sets pri -son-ers      free.
the Lord, who                 loves the   just,        the Lord, who pro   -   tects the stranger.
The Lord will                 reign for   ever,        Zion's God, from            age  to      age.

# Psalm 146 (147) – The wisdom of God in creation

vv. 1-6. R/ v. 3

5th Sunday in Ordinary Time (Year B)

*Response:* **Praise** the Lord who heals the bro - - ken - heart-ed.

1. Praise the Lord for he is good;    sing to our God for he is loving:
2. The Lord builds    up Je-rusalem    and brings back Is - ra-el's exiles,
3. Our Lord is great    and al-mighty;    his wisdom can nev-er be measured.

[                              ]
he heals the bro-ken-hearted,    he binds up all their wounds.
[                              ]

*This line for verse 2 only*

[                              ]
He fixes the number of the stars;    to him our    praise is due.
The Lord rai - ses the low-ly;    he calls each one    by its name.
    he humbles the wicked    to the dust.

*Omit phrase in verse 1*

# Psalm 147 - Praise of God's care for Israel

## vv. 12-15, 19-20

2nd Sunday after Christmas – response 1 (Jn 1:14)
Corpus Christi (year A) – response 2 (v. 12)

*Response 1 (Christmastide):* **The Word was made flesh, and lived_ a- mong us.**

*Response 2 (Corpus Christi):* **O praise the Lord,__ Je - ru - - sa - lem!**

*\* – The first phrase ('O...Jerusalem') is optional on Corpus Christi*

1. *O praise the Lord, Je - rusalem! Zion, praise__ your God!
2. He established peace on your borders, he feeds you with fi - nest wheat.
3. He makes his word known to Jacob, to Israel his laws and de - crees.

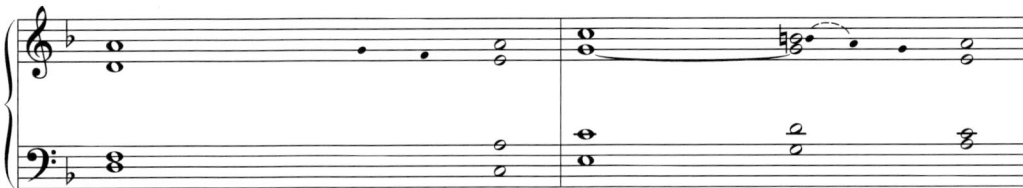

He has strengthened the bars of your gates, he has blessed the child-ren with-in you.
He sends out his word to the earth and swiftly runs his com-mand.
He has not dealt thus with oth - er nations; he has not taught them his de - crees.

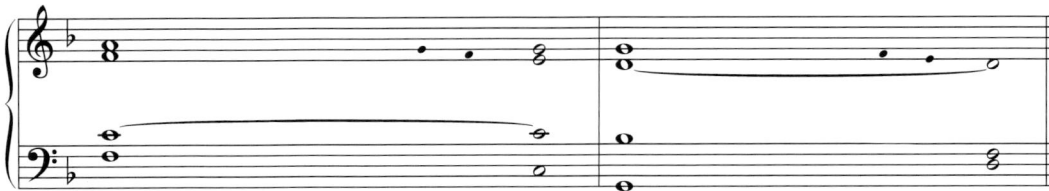

*Let everything that lives and that breathes*
*give praise to the Lord. Alleluia!*

*Psalm 150:6*
*The Conclusion of the Book of Psalms*

126

# CANTICLES

# Exodus 15 – The Passover Song of Moses

vv. 1-6, 17-18. R/ v. 1

Easter Vigil (after the 3rd reading)

*Note: This canticle follows the reading without a break*

*Response:* **I will sing to the Lord, glo-rious his tri-umph!**

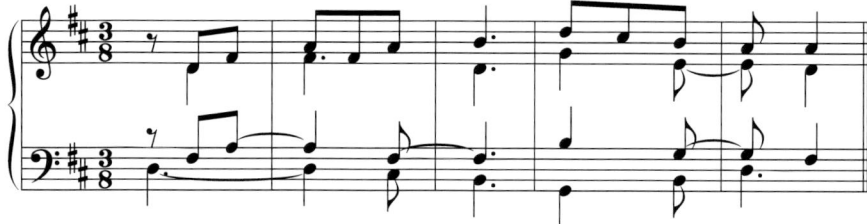

1. Horse and ri-der he has thrown in - to the sea!
2. The Lord is a warrior! The Lord is his name.
3. Your right hand, Lord, glorious in its power,
4. You will lead your people and plant them on your mountain,

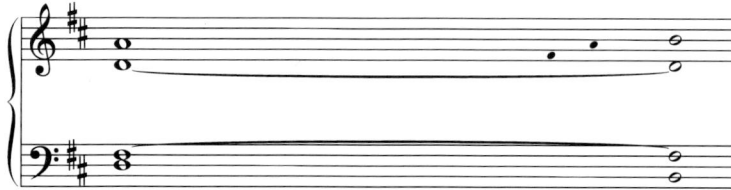

The Lord is my strength, my song, my sal-vation.
The chariots of Pharaoh he hurled in - to the sea,
your right hand, Lord, has shat - tered the enemy.
the place, O Lord, where you have made your home,

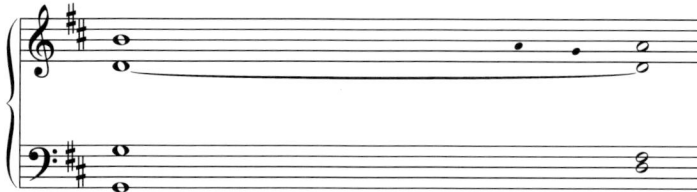

This is my God and I ex - tol him,
the flower of his army is drowned in the sea.
[                                                    ]
the sanctuary, Lord, which your hands have made.

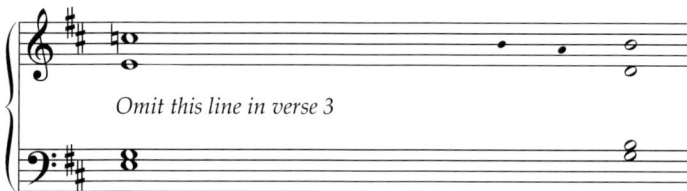

*Omit this line in verse 3*

my father's God and I give him praise.
The deeps hide them; they sank like a stone.
In the greatness of your glory you crushed the foe.
The Lord will reign for ev - er and ever.

# Isaiah 12

## vv. 2-6

Easter Vigil (after the 5th reading) – response 1 (v 3)
Baptism of the Lord (Year B option) – response 1 (v. 3)
Sacred Heart (Year B) – response 1 (v. 3)
3rd Sunday of Advent (Year C) – response 2 (v. 6)

*Response 1:* **With** joy you will draw wa - - ter from the wells of sal - va - - tion.

*Response 2:* **Sing and shout** for joy for great in your midst is the Ho - ly One of Is - - ra-el.

1. Truly, God is my sal-vation, I trust, I shall not fear.
2. Give thanks to the Lord, give praise to his name!
3. Sing a psalm to the Lord, for he has done glo -ri-ous deeds, make them known to all the earth!

For the Lord is my strength, my song, he be - came my saviour.
Make his mighty deeds known to the peoples! Declare the greatness of his name.
People of Zion, sing and shout for joy for great in your midst is the Holy One of Israel.

# Daniel 3 – The Song in the Fiery Furnace

vv. 52-56. R/ v.52

Pentecost Vigil (after the 2nd reading)
Trinity Sunday (Year A)

*Response:* **To you glo-ry and praise for ev - er - more.**

1. You are blest, Lord God      of   our  fathers.   **To you...**
2. Blest your glorious          ho - ly   name.
3. You are blest in the temple  of   your   glory.
4. You are blest on the throne  of   your kingdom.
5. You are blest who gaze in - to   the   depths.
6. You are blest in the firma - ment  of   heaven.

# The Magnificat

Lk 1:46-55. R/ Is 61:10

3rd Sunday of Advent (Year B)

*Response:* **My soul___ re - joi - - ces___ in___ my___ God.**

*\* – This verse is not given in the Lectionary, but is printed here for the sake of completeness.*

1. My soul glori - fies the Lord, my spirit rejoices in God, my Saviour.
2. The Almighty works mar-vels for me. Ho - ly his name!
*2a. He puts forth his arm in strength and scatters the proud-hearted.
3. He fills the star - ving with good things, sends the rich a - way empty.

He looks on his servant in her lowliness; henceforth all ages will call me blessèd.
His mercy is from age to age on those who fear him.
He casts the mighty from their thrones and rais - es the lowly.
He protects Isra - el, his servant, remember - ing his [ ] mercy,

1, 2, 2a        3

*The following ending for verse 3 is not given in the Lectionary.*

the mercy promised to our fathers, to Abraham and his sons for ever.

# APPENDIX:
# GOSPEL ACCLAMATIONS

## Gospel Acclamation: liturgical purpose

The Gospel Acclamation performs a liturgical function entirely different to that of the Responsorial Psalm.

It is the Gospel Procession that is the liturgical action to which the participants' attention should be drawn – even if it is just a priest or deacon processing to the ambo by himself. The Gospel Acclamation is the accompaniment to the procession. It is best led by a vocal group or cantor distinct from the psalmist who has sung the psalm. If the same cantor has sung the psalm, s/he should remove from the ambo before leading the Gospel Acclamation, since the ambo is now the destination of the Gospel Procession.

The Gospel Acclamation is normally 'Alleluia', often repeated; but 'Alleluia' is never sung in Lent, or in the Sacred Triduum before the first Easter Alleluia at the Easter Vigil. For these times, the Lectionary provides a selection of alternative acclamation texts.

It is normal for the congregation to repeat the acclamation initially after the vocal group or cantor, though it may well join in a well-known setting after the first Alleluia, or spontaneously, in which case a repeat may not be necessary. All repeat the acclamation after the verse, which is normally sung by the vocal group or cantor.

## Some simple settings

A variety of simple settings is given below.

The texts for the Gospel Acclamation verse can be found in the Lectionary or in a Sunday Missal. Since this varies from day to day, a simple psalm-tone is provided for each setting. The group or cantor should prepare the words for singing beforehand. Many Gospel Acclamation verses fall naturally into two lines; where there are three, a pause on the reciting note may be made after the first line.

All the settings below require the cadence of each half to begin two syllables before the last accented syllable of the line.

## THROUGHOUT THE YEAR (EXCEPT LENT)

Al-le-lu - - ia,    al-le-lu - - ia,    al-le-lu - - ia!

Al - - le-lu - - ia,    al - - le-lu - - ia,    al - - le-lu - - ia!

Al-le-lu - - ia,    al-le-lu - - ia,    al-le-lu - - ia!

Al-le-lu - - ia,    al-le-lu - - - ia,    al - - le-lu - ia!

Al-le-lu - - ia,    al - - le-lu - - ia,    al - - le-lu - ia!

Al-le-lu-ia,    al - - le-lu - ia,___    al-le - - lu - - ia!

Al-le-lu - -ia, al-le-lu - -ia, al-le-lu - -ia!

Al - -le-lu - -ia, al-le-lu - - ia, al - -le-lu - -ia!

## DURING LENT (AND MAUNDY THURSDAY, GOOD FRIDAY)

Praise to you, O Christ, king of e-ter-nal glo-ry!

Glo-ry and praise to you, O Christ!

Glo-ry to you, O Christ, you are the Word__ of God!

Praise__ and hon-our to you, Lord__ Je - sus!

# LITURGICAL INDEX

## PROPER OF TIME

*Page Numbers*

| Year A | Year B | Year C | |
|---|---|---|---|
| | | | Advent: |
| 108 | 66 | 22 | 1st Sunday |
| 62 | 69 | 111 | 2nd Sunday |
| 123 | 131 | 129 | 3rd Sunday |
| 18 | 72 | 66 | 4th Sunday |
| | | | Christmas: |
| 70 | 70 | 70 | Vigil |
| 79 | 79 | 79 | Night |
| 81 | 81 | 81 | Dawn |
| 83 | 83 | 83 | Day |
| 112 | 92* | 68* | Holy Family |
| 56 | 56 | 56 | Mary Mother |
| 126 | 126 | 126 | 2nd Sunday after Christmas |
| | | | Epiphany: |
| 61 | 61 | 61 | Vigil |
| 61 | 61 | 61 | Day |
| 27 | 129* | 90* | Baptism of the Lord |
| | | | |
| 49 | 49 | 49 | Ash Wednesday |
| | | | Lent: |
| 49 | 20 | 75 | 1st Sunday |
| 33 | 98 | 24 | 2nd Sunday |
| 78 | 11 | 87 | 3rd Sunday |
| 16 | 117 | 37 | 4th Sunday |
| 113 | 50 | 111 | 5th Sunday |
| 14 | 14 | 14 | Palm Sunday |

*All Years*

| | | |
|---|---|---|
| 99 | | Maundy Thursday |
| 29 | | Good Friday |
| | | Easter Vigil: |
| 89 | | 1st Psalm |
| 35 | | 1st Psalm (alternative) |
| 7 | | 2nd Psalm |
| 128 | | 3rd Psalm |
| 28 | | 4th Psalm |
| 129 | | 5th Psalm |
| 11 | | 6th Psalm |
| 44 | | 7th Psalm |
| 50 | | 7th Psalm (alternative) |
| 101 | | Alleluia Psalm |
| 102 | | Easter Sunday |

| Year A | Year B | Year C | |
|---|---|---|---|
| | | | Sundays of Easter: |
| 102 | 102 | 104 | 2nd Sunday of Easter |
| 8 | 4 | 28 | 3rd Sunday of Easter |
| 16 | 105 | 85 | 4th Sunday of Easter |
| 34 | 15 | 122 | 5th Sunday of Easter |
| 55 | 84 | 56 | 6th Sunday of Easter |
| 47 | 47 | 47 | Ascension Day |
| 23 | 87 | 82 | 7th Sunday of Easter |

\* - The year A psalm may be substituted.

## COMMON PSALMS

*These seasonal psalms may replace the psalm proper to a Sunday.*

| | |
|---|---|
| 22, 69 | Advent |
| 83 | Christmas |
| 61 | Epiphany |
| 49, 75, 113 | Lent |
| 14 | Holy Week |
| 116 | Easter Vigil |
| 102, 55 | Easter Season |
| 47 | Ascension |
| 91 | Pentecost |
| 11, 24, 37, 53, 78, 85, 87, 120 | Ordinary Time |
| 108 | Ordinary Time (last weeks of the year) |

## PROPER OF SAINTS

| | |
|---|---|
| 19 | February 2: The Presentation of the Lord |
| 2 | March 1: St David (in Wales) |
| 100 | March 17: St Patrick (in Ireland) |
| 72 | March 19: St Joseph |
| 40 | March 25: The Annunciation of the BVM |
| 111 | April 23: St George (in England) |
| 60 | June 23: St John the Baptist (Vigil) |
| 119 | June 24: St John the Baptist (Day) |
| 13 | June 28: SS Peter & Paul (Vigil) |
| 37 | June 29: SS Peter & Paul (Day) |
| 82 | August 6: The Transfiguration of the Lord |
| 115 | August 14: The Assumption of the BVM (Vigil) |
| 45 | August 15: The Assumption of the BVM (Day) |
| 65 | September 14: The Triumph of the Cross |
| 18 | November 1: All Saints |
| 25 | November 2: All Souls |
| 46 | November 9: Dedication of the Lateran Basilica |
| 31 | November 30: St Andrew (in Scotland) |
| 83 | December 8: The Immaculate Conception of the BVM |
| 68 | Anniversary of Dedication |